African Centered Rites of Passage

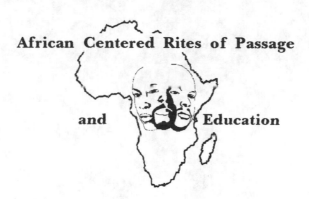

and  Education

Lathardus Goggins II

Chicago, Illinois

Cover design by Lathardus Goggins II & Orlando Lewis
Photo by Kevin Goode
Copyright © 1996 by Lathardus Goggins II
First Edition, First Printing

Printed in the United States of America

ISBN: 0-913543-49-7

TABLE OF CONTENTS

WRN

ACKNOWLEDGMENTS

All honor and praise to the Creator of us all, the original ancestor from whom all blessings, wisdom, and power flow.

Hallelujah-Asante sana Jesus, for your saving grace and mercy.

Asante sana to the ancestors. It is on their blood, work, and prayers we stand.

Let us remember the people who sacrificed their lives and those who were killed during our struggle.

Let us mourn the lost potential of the millions who perished during the middle passage, the thousands who died due to the brutality of American oppression, and the daily slaughter by those whose minds are in the hands of the oppressor.

Asante sana to the community elders and scholars who have provided guidance and have reminded us of our true selves.

Asante sana to all those who provided wisdom and support in the writing of this book: especially Mama, Pops, my wife Dietra, Carla, Luzby, Robin, "Mike," "Donna," "Jon," "Joan," "Anna," T. Shelton, A. Bilal, Kwame Scruggs, Aunt Annie-Mae, Aunt Zee, V. Seeberg, K. Durgans, N. Oliver, M. Scott, S. Lee, E. Baylock, D. Wilcox, Pastor Fowler, J. Harkness, M. Kemp, and A. Sample.

Let us remember the unborn and persons new to the earth. Let all that we do lead them to the knowing of God, the knowing of authentic self, and fulfillment of purpose.

Ashe!

Dedicated to Lathardus Goggins III (Trè)

The United States and colonial Africa have educated [schooled] African people into dependency.

John Henrik Clarke

The greatest weapon in the hands of the oppressor is the mind of the oppressed.

Steve Biko

Chance has never yet satisfied the hope of a suffering people. Action, self-reliance, the vision of self, and the future have been the only means by which the oppressed have seen and realized the light of their own freedom.

Marcus Garvey

I would never be of any service to any one as a slave. . . . The manner in which I learned to read and write, had a great influence on my own mind.

Nat Turner

Education is our passport to the future, for tomorrow belongs to the people who prepare for it today.

El Hajj Malik El Shabazz

Education is a tool to independency.

Moses L. Osborne

INTRODUCTION

It is said that the second structure built by the Pilgrims was a schoolhouse. The concept of education has been at the heart of the American experience. Goldschmidt (1977, p. 137) defines education as the process by which both obvious aspects of culture and its hidden minutiae are transmitted from one generation to another. Education is also the process that prepares the young for their future membership and active participation in the maintenance or development of a society (Nyerere, 1967). Paulo Freire (1970) argues, in *Pedagogy of the Oppressed*, that there is no such thing as a neutral education; it is not the transfer of objective information. Education is laced with values, social norms, and perceptions. In the United States, these "obvious and hidden aspects of culture" are predominately based on a white European male Protestant supremacy (WEMPS) worldview (Boykin, 1986; Hale-Benson, 1986; Knowles & Prewitt, 1969; Spindler & Spindler, 1990).

Race, gender, and socioeconomic status are other issues at the center of the American experience, resulting in a number of educational systems structured to perpetuate social norms and prepare individuals to fulfill social needs. However, for the purpose of this study I will focus on the educational systems for African Americans.[1]

[1.] *African, African American, Afro-American, Black, black, Negro, colored*: These terms are often synonymous. The term used is a function of the time period of the work or the philosophy of the author. Transition from Colored to African or African American is reflective of the redefining of people of African descent in the United States. For this study the term of choice is African American. However, Africans will be used when referring to people of African descent prior to the Fourteenth amendment. Black (capitalized) refers to state of mind or ethnic group, while black denotes race.

Mainstream America's perceptions of African American deficiencies and white supremacy have produced educational systems that have served different purposes. Generally, European Americans are prepared to assume positions of power in society, while African Americans are prepared to fill subordinate positions (Irvine, 1991; Montgomery et al., 1993; Ogbu, 1974, 1986; Warfield-Coppock, 1992). Therefore, any discussion of the academic performance of African Americans must first consider the dynamics between the mainstream and people of African descent (Boykin, 1986; Cress-Welsing, 1991). W. E. B. Du Bois (1903/1965) in the classic *The Souls of Black Folk* and A.W. Boykin (1986) in "The Triple Quandary and the Schooling of Afro-American Children" discuss the effects of "the obvious aspects and hidden minutiae" on the consciousness of African Americans, which often result in lower academic performance.

The low academic success of African Americans in the United States has been well documented; explanations for this performance have ranged from low genetic endowment to a function of the white educational system. However, Grambs (1963) suggests that the American race caste system tends to foster development of a conception of self in African American students which results in poor academic development. Ogbu (1974, 1986) furthers this argument. He has identified low academic performance as a similarity of "castelike minorities" in various societies around the world, even when the castelike minority group is of the same race as the dominant class. Ogbu suggests that the academic performance of African Americans is not a function of genetics or of being in a white educational system but is a function of castelike minority status.

Such coping skills as hopelessness, dropping out, surviving, dissembling, getting over, racelessness, selling out, and oppositional cultures have developed among African American students as a response to an oppressive school system (Boykin, 1986; Fordham, 1988; Freire, 1970; Ogbu, 1974, 1986). However, cognitive factors such as an ability to deal with racism, realistic self-appraisal, and positive self-concept have been found to be important factors predicting the academic success of African Americans (Tracey & Sedlacek, 1985).

The importance of knowing oneself is an axiom that both ancient and modern scholars have recognized. The proverb Man Know Thyself was written on the walls of learning centers in ancient Kemet (Egypt) (Akbar, 1985; Hilliard et al., 1987). Sun-tzu (6th cent. B.C./1988) stated in *The Art of War*:

> If you know others and know yourself, you will not be
> endangered in a hundred battles; if you do not know
> others but know yourself, for every battle won, you will
> lose one; if you do not know others and do not know
> yourself, you will be endangered in every battle.

(Note: Sun-tzu does not consider the possibility of not knowing self but knowing others.) Modern scholars reiterate that the knowledge of self is the base from which one understands the world (Akbar, 1985; Asante, 1987; Wilson, 1987). Proponents of progressive education such as Dewey, Woodson, Freire, and Hale-Benson have suggested that a student's sense of self is an essential part in determining whether an experience is educative or mis-educative. Other scholars who have developed various models to predict academic performance or show the cognitive process either directly or indirectly imply that a student must have developed some sense of self. The literature suggests that a failure to develop cultural awareness or cultural self-consciousness, may have a negative impact on academic achievement (Durgans, 1992).

To ensure the development of cultural self-consciousness, many societies provide rituals and ceremonies that symbolize and transfer the collective wisdom of that culture (Cohen, 1991). These rites of passage occur at significant moments, when individuals pass from one state of being to the next (Cohen, 1991; Hare & Hare, 1985; Hill, 1992; Perkins, 1986; Somè, 1994; van Gennep, 1908/1960; Warfield-Coppock, 1992, 1994). Each next state coincides with expected responsibilities and consciousness of self and others. It is through the rites that a society/culture provides its members with the following: (a) historical continuity, (b) responsibilities, and (c) a functional rationale of the world.

Specifically, African-centered rites of passage are rituals and ceremonies based on such African concepts as spirituality, communalism, expressive individualism, reciprocity, and intergenerational balance. The rituals and ceremonies are designed to help initiates find and develop purpose, to link initiates to the African community, and to help initiates find their true personality i.e., to develop a sense of self. It is this sense of self that is the context in which one makes meaning.

Problem Statement

The paradox is that African American students, having castelike minority status, must achieve academic success in a school system which transfers and embodies the values and purpose of the oppressor. Yet in order to achieve, African American students must garner and maintain a positive sense of self (Kunjufu, 1986). A process needs to be identified that will allow African American students to interact with a socially, culturally, and psychologically hostile system and still be academically successful and maintain a positive sense of self.

My research will examine the possibility of African centered rites of passage as a factor in positive academic success. Central to this study are the arguments for progressive education made by Dewey (1938/1968), Freire (1970), and Woodson (1933/1990). However, the focus is not on the need for change in the system, but the need for development of self.

Methodology

This study will be heuristic in nature. According to Gore (1964), the essential function of the heuristic process is to induce a several-sided, commonly held set of understandings consisting of a shared conception of the world in general, the problem at hand, and the conditions under which the problem can be acceptably resolved from the jumble of conceptions that constitute the normal state of affairs, which represent a collective consensus. This study will attempt to draw a consensus from the scholarly literature and narratives relevant to the socialization, construction of self-concept, and education of African Americans. The following questions served as scaffolding for this discussion:

1. How is sense of self dealt with in rites of passage, and specifically within African centered rites of passage?

2. What is the theory regarding the construction of self and its relationship to the educative experience?

3. What are the operating assumptions about educating African Americans?

4. In what ways do the rites of passage influence the educative experience?

Starting with such classics as Du Bois's (1903/1965) *The Souls of Black Folk*, Woodson's (1933/1990) *The Mis-Education of the Negro*, and Freire's (1970) *Pedagogy of the Oppressed*, I examined the literature for common themes. The emerging themes from previous readings became the criteria for subsequent readings. This parallels Freire's (1970) argument for praxis (reflection and action), the means by which the oppressed develop pedagogy.

CHAPTER 1

RITES OF PASSAGE

General Definition

All cultures/societies have some kind of rites of passage to ensure cultural self-consciousness (Campbell, 1949/1973; Cohen, 1991; van Gennep, 1908/1960). Rites of passage appear to be universal, a part of human consciousness (Macintosh, 1995; Shere, 1993; van Gennep, 1908/1960). Rites of passage rituals and ceremonies represent the collective wisdom of a culture/society (Cohen, 1991; Warfield-Coppock, 1994). These rituals and ceremonies mark the transition from one stage/category of life to another (Quinn, Newfield, & Protinsky, 1985; van Gennep, 1908/1960; Warfield-Coppock, 1994). There are rites for biological, philosophical, and social passages, such as birth, puberty, death, marriage, adulthood, organizations, and self-consciousness (van Gennep, 1908/1960). Along with marking various stages of life, the rites imply changes in responsibilities and expectations (Somè, 1994; Quinn, Newfield, & Protinsky, 1985; van Gennep, 1908/1960). In *Rituals,* Somè (1993) describes ceremony as the anatomy of ritual. Ceremonies are visual representations of what happens as a result of the ritual. Thus the quality of the ritual is embedded in the intent of the ceremony. Therefore, purpose is the factor that contributes to the effectiveness of ritual. Somè also asserts that there are three types of rituals: (1) Communal, (2) Family, and (3) Individual.

Communal rituals affirm unity and cohesiveness. Every adult member of the village is obligated to attend.

Family rituals provide unity and cohesiveness for family units and are performed by family elders. All responsible family members, those initiated into adulthood, are expected to attend.

Individual rituals are those rituals which individuals must perform to maintain a proper relationship with the cosmos.

Communal, family, and individual rituals are interdependent and provide consistency between community, family, and individual responsibilities. By performing these rituals, the initiates demonstrate their ability to fulfill their responsibilities within that culture/society. This may explain why the transitions from adolescence to adulthood and marriage tend to be the most elaborate ceremonies. As mentioned earlier, there are many different kinds of rites of passage, consisting of a variety of rituals. However, for the purpose of this study, *rites of passage* refers to family-based and community-linked rituals that are designed to mark the transition from one stage of life to the next and provide the necessary tenets to fulfill purpose and responsibilities within a culture/society. It should also be noted that the rites of passage process, not a description of the ceremonies, is the focus of this discussion.

The rites of passage process is a pattern of preparation, separation, transition, and reincorporation (Cohen, 1991; Hare, 1985; Hill, 1992; M.E.C.C.A., n.d; Somè, 1994; van Gennep, 1908/1960). The significance of the pattern is in the fostering of continuity. Preparation is when the initiates learn what it is to be a member of that society/culture and develop an understanding of necessary skills, responsibilities, and expectations in order to fulfill their purpose within the culture/society and stage of life. Separation is when the initiate demonstrates the ability to perform expected skills and responsibilities. Transition is the phase that one enters as a nonmember and emerges as a member. Reincorporation is when the new members are accepted back into the culture/society by elders and expected to carry out their purpose within the culture/society, thereby maintaining it. The cycle is repeated for the next passage. What was the reincorporation for the previous passage becomes the preparation for the next passage. This process creates an experiential continuum, which is educative (Dewey, 1938/1963). The rites of passage process establishes (1) collective cohesiveness of action among the members, (2) a framework of expectations for the participants, and (3) a cognitive map for responding to stressors (Quinn, Newfield, & Protinsky, 1985).

Interview Data

I conducted three interviews in order to better understand: (1) the purpose of rites of passage in general and specifically in the African American community, and (2) to gain further insight into how self-concept and education influence rites of passage. I interviewed five people familiar with rites of passage whom I will call Jon, Joan, Anna, Mike and Donna. Jon, Joan, Anna are Jewish, and Mike and Donna are African Americans. My primary assumptions were that African Americans and Jews have had similar experiences in terms of slavery, oppression, and discrimination. Since African Americans and Jews have experienced similar oppression, parallels can be drawn between the rites of passage of both in terms of purpose and expected self-development. I expected themes of linkage (connectedness to community, family, and creator); understanding the situations people find themselves in; defining purpose; strategy; self-consciousness; transition from one stage to another and the expected responsibilities with each stage; and finding purpose based on community needs, which leads to academic success, the ability to deal with hostile situations, and self- esteem.

I interviewed Jon, Joan, and Anna together. A number of themes emerged throughout the interview. However, most of them could be categorized as continuity, the importance of family, expectations, and cultural self-consciousness. The following are some examples:

Joan: Your whole historical memory is that you were a slave. And don't ever think that it happened 3,500 years ago. Feel as if it happened to you. That you are a witness. Just like you feel that you are a witness when Moses came and gave the Torah and he said the words, I know it by heart.

You are standing before me with your children and their children and your families and your grand-children, but not only you that are here but all the generations to come for many thousands of years in the future.

In the Jewish experience you are not only expected to know the history, you are expected to be a witness to it. You are not only expected to know that Moses received the Ten Commandments but as a Jew you are expected to be a witness to that event, and therefore all the responsibilities that were told to Moses were told to you; and with these responsibilities comes accountability.

Jon: Bar Mitzvah means "son of the commandments." He's responsible, on his own. Judgment is coming from himself; the parents are not responsible for his sins or good deeds anymore.

Anna: Along with it there are several burdens, too, because we have great expectations for our children. You know, I think a lot of times our children feel that they are driven, because of the responsibilities that we have placed on them. The Bar Mitzvah and the Bas Mitzvah are perfect examples because of the responsibilities that children must accept for that service, and the meaning behind the service, so that once they complete that process, the learning process, then they are legitimate carriers-on of the tradition. They are

4

able to then be a part of the community, the religious community in conducting services and being part of the Minion. So it's a tremendous responsibility, and it's not taken lightly. I think it's typical of a Jewish parent, the way we rear our children, and our values. There are things I know, with my children growing up, that they would say to me, "Why do I have to study so hard? The kids in my class don't have to." And I would say "Because you are working toward a future. You have responsibilities."

Expectations or burdens do not start with the Bar/Bas Mitzvah, but were placed on the children at birth.

Joan: It's symbolic. And it's interesting that in the time of this ceremony, the Rabbi or whoever does this particular ceremony, he says, "This child, it is the eighth day." They do it after the eighth day, to make sure the child is alive and has some strength. They say, "Thirteen years from today, it will be Bar Mitzvah." And we talked about the Bar Mitzvah. And he's still approached with such and such. They announce already that it will be his responsibility to do the reading, because every week he will read the Torah. He will read, I know that on my birthday, every year at that day includes this Torah. So my grandson is going to be Bar Mitzvah in June. We know exactly their birthday, and I look at the calendar and I know it is Torah this week. In the Bar Mitzvah, they say he will read, they say like that (Hebrew), which means "the little one will grow to be a big one."

From birth, they know that when it comes to Bar Mitzvah that this child will be expected to read from the particular section of the Torah. This is the foundation for which Hebrew school and Jewish education become necessary (McConnell, 1989; Shade, 1989). This is consistent with the argument made by John Dewey (1938/1963) in *Experience and Education*. Dewey suggested that an experiential continuum was a criterion for determining whether an experience was educative or mis-educative. If an experience is disconnected, does not draw on the past to build a future, then it is mis-educative. Also, one can not expect self-control in disconnected experiences. So, in the case of Jews, the life cycle provides the experiential continuum that makes self-control and discipline meaningful.

Anna: ". . . you are working towards a future."

The importance of family was another theme,

Anna: The most important thing in Judaism is the family. It's the raising of the children, the love, the nurturing, the teaching, all these things are very, very important. We do not take them lightly.

Joan: The family is the first unit of education. It is repeated in every way possible from the beginning of time. The responsibility of the parent is to teach the youth and the children. . .

Jon gave some insight into how Jews deal with living in foreign or hostile societies.

My point of view is that we have not adopted any other culture, but in doing this we're trying to live our culture in the general society . . . being able to live in the same society, our way, and being a part of the other general community in a positive way. We're not saying we don't have to give up ours, and we don't have to build ours up enough, but we are and we need to adjust and be able to function in that society. Many times we would say it is the same as to say we should be: I'm going to put it in simple terms, to have a Jewish home in an American society.

Jon's narrative suggests that there is a filter that must be used to determine the meaning of a situation. There is a Jewish standard which one is expected to examine the world critically. This is reflective of the difference between involuntary and voluntary minorities suggested by Ogbu (1991). Voluntary minorities tend to have some measure of academic success, because they are able to define and understand their place within a society. It should be noted that Ogbu (1974, 1986) describes Jews as autonomous minorities and makes a distinction between them and voluntary minorities like the Chinese and Koreans. However, Ogbu (1986) does suggest that both autonomous and voluntary minorities tend to use cultural models and frames of reference that encourage success.

For the interviews discussing African centered rites of passage, I selected two people who are familiar with the Akan Tradition Model of Anthony Mensah. Donna had recently been initiated into rites, less than two months previously. She had dropped out of high school to get married. At present she is a mother of two, divorced, and a college student. I hoped she would contribute perceptions of a parent, a student, and a new initiate. Mike is a member of the *kollective* that has been involved in formal rites of passage for about four years. He is a father of two, married, and a professional. I hoped to gain insight from a person that had been involved with rites long enough for it to have a lasting impact. Mike was not initiated into the same kollective as Donna. It was my assumption, given their different situations and length of involvement, that each will have a different perspective. However, I did expect some continuity in their discussions: themes like linkage to community "fictive kinship" (Fordham, 1988), and having a sense of mission/purpose.

Each interview was scheduled at the convenience of the interviewee. I asked them both: (1) How would you define rites of passage? (2) How has rites of passage affected you? and (3) What do you think of the education system? Based on their responses I then asked other probing questions. The following were their responses.

1. How would you define rites of passage?

Donna: Hum. Without using the definitions, I would describe it as something that helps a person do exactly what the definition of it is, which is to help a person go from one life situation to the next smoothly, basically. And to make that transition a little better than it would have been had you not been conscious of the things that take place in your life, whatever, good or bad, and how you handle them.

Mike: Rites of Passage is a way of life. It's a focus; it's a centeredness of you knowing who you are and how you tie into everything else that goes on. You see your linkage with the whole cosmos down to the simple neighbor on the street. So the term rites of passage is the process of transition from one stage to the next. It's an order; it's a balance, taking natural forces into consideration, as opposed to social forces and influences that may not lead to the best end. And that's a lot of where I'm coming from. But rites of passage is a bigger end in store for everybody. And that's what rites of passage has offered me, that insight, that foresight to realize that definition that describes all of us, the realization that I cannot achieve what others don't achieve. We're all in this together.

Defining rites of passage similarly would be expected, given that both have been initiated into the same model. However, there were some differences. Donna emphasized the idea of transition and has focused specifically on her family, while Mike concentrated on linkage and societal issues. These themes were constant throughout their respective interviews.

2. How has rites of passage affected you?

Donna: To me, I'm becoming more conscious of myself, things that I should do that I don't do, things that I do, that I should not do. For example, everybody does it, and you don't feel like going to it, but you make yourself go. Working two jobs is not easy, and I have to do that because it's just me. I'd like to think I've always been an open-minded person. An open-hearted person. I'd like to think that is something that's been in me, and that will continue to be in me and will enhance me.

Mike: I was a victim of I'm O.K., you're O.K., the whole Freudian trend. I was in there with these schools, so I am totally aware of it. However, rites of passage brought me back to the community that could answer those questions. And I was always aware of the fact that I could pursue higher educational levels, as I explained before. Rites gave me a means of knowing who I was first. Before I could see anything else, I needed to know who I was first. Therefore, when I digested that information from a knowledgeable individual, as opposed to what I may conceptualize, I began to understand who I was first. Therefore, when the information came in, I understood it.

3. What do you think of the education system?

Donna: I think it sucks. The reason I think that, is because it doesn't take the time to find out what the needs of the individual child are, and it doesn't provide those needs. Right now, we look at things totally politically, and that's not the way they should be looked at, you think about it. . . I see that in all forms of education and institutions and environment when it comes to them not giving their best, the instructors. That's discouraging to students, and it limits the student because they have no idea what their potential is. And right now, our school systems, for the most part, it's not to say that all schools are bad, but the whole educational system is totally messed up. However, we have major problems.

Mike: To me, education is inevitable. It's something you can't get around anywhere. Visually or audibly, your learning returns. It's to see something different. You're picking up something new all the time. The academic educational arena, I worry sometimes about that, because the curriculum is being used to create a product in the end. If I just use the whole capitalist system as an example, and I try to tell African Americans this all the time, if they produce in your company the same kind of product that's coming out of the schools, why are we still going to public schools? If a product came out that defective, who would buy that product? Simple analogy. No one would; and the people who produce it, they would be fired. There is no way that they could still hold their job. That's their system.

Donna and Mike answered the basic questions very similarly, though their emphases were different. Self-development and tenets of progressive education were also apparent in their responses to the basic questions. When answering probing questions, many of the same themes emerged as well:

1. Linkage/Connectedness to community, family and Creator:

Donna: Connectedness to her daughter, connectedness to her brother, connectedness to her people. To her creator, to everything that she needs to be connected to, as opposed to the thingsthat she doesn't need to be connected to.

Mike: Rites of passage is a term, they should realize, that we are all tied in. If any one of my brothers or sisters is hurt, then I'm hurting. If anyone is homeless, then I must also feel those pains. No matter where they are on the planet. That's the focus of our agenda.

2. Understanding the situations in which one finds oneself:

Donna: What does rites of passage mean to me? It's helped me to understand the changes that I've been through. I may not grasp them right away, but it helps me to understand those changes, and it helps me to go through them better.

Mike: You could still get the understanding of what we were. So that's the whole thought process. But I must maintain who I originally was. I must do that. Then, I'll understand who they were.

3. Defining purpose and strategy:

Donna: It helps me to cope better with everything. . . . I'm totally aware of the fact that there's a purpose for everything.

11

Mike: They have bought into the American dream to the extent that they no longer know the realities of thought. Even to say "I want a piece of the pie" is to say that they have already just given in to a system. You've already said, this is the only pie. I want my own pie. No thanks, I can make my own. Black people, we need our academics. The Jewish environment, I know that a major part of their life is not what they learn in schools. I know that. A large part of their academics and their academic environment they learn outside of the American school system. African Americans depend on their academic answers in the school system. And it's foolish. And they don't realize that it's an accumulation of everything, it's your whole environment, your home, your church, it's your society, your neighborhood, all that is building who that person must become.

4. Self-consciousness:

Donna: With maturity, yes. I would also say it has something to do with an appreciation for who his son is, who he understands himself to be. And where he came from and where he's going. And where he wants to go.

Mike: I must walk a certain way, and deal with whatever frailties I have. Oh, I have my problems, my vices, I'm still a warrior. The success has come because I know the Creator is saying I have something for you to do.

5. Academic success based on one's purpose and community needs:

Donna: We can all get a better education, a better understanding. Because they don't teach the truth in schools. And they don't necessarily teach things that are necessary for you to make it in your daily life, even on the job!

Mike: Prepare yourself for that particular mission. . . . That is the whole academic role, the rites, the Afrocentric tradition.

6. Low teacher/system expectation (schooling system was not instituted for African Americans' benefit):

Donna: And you also need to have the truth in the textbooks for whatever subject it is. That aids with diversity, cultural diversity. You need to be honest, totally. That way, we can all get a better education, a better understanding. Because they don't teach the truth in schools. And they don't necessarily teach things that are necessary for you to make it in your daily life, even on the job!

Mike: Rites will tell them, help me to become a young man, understand who you are and that you are in a battle zone, so you must protect yourself. These are the kinds of tactics that you most need. Do not go there thinking that the [school] system is going to afford you the same opportunities that it affords them. You were not written into that original blueprint. You were added later on.

7. The need for parental and community involvement in the education of children:

Donna: She has been informed that it is probably best for her to start up again. [Goggins: Informed by whom?] By her mother. [Goggins: What do you expect, why would you assume that it (rites) would be best for her?] Why would I assume that it would be best? It will help to ground her. It will help her to have some understanding, some guidance, some appreciation, connectedness. And all of that is necessary.

Mike: With our kids, Afrocentrically, we need to be aware. And they are not aware of their true purpose. We allow stuff to happen.

Mike discussed other concepts, such as informal rites of passage, using different values from the oppressor to ensure a different outcome, Sankofa (learning from history to correct today's problems) and courage. Mike shared a "call and response" that captures the essence of both interviews:

> I talk to them, "Black child, Black child, what are you going to do?" And their response is, "Whatever my people need from me." I ask them, "How and why?" They say, "I can be what I want to be, if I try to be the best that I can be, and I will be!" The key is nature, your life circumstances, is cause for you to be accountable. It is calling.

The narrative of the participants suggests there are some basic concepts shared by the Jewish Life Cycle and African centered rites of passage. However, there were some significant differences. One difference implied was between concepts of finding oneself versus being oneself. Within the Jewish experience, the person does not find himself/herself, he/she has already been found. The rituals and ceremonies are a part of being Jewish. The rituals and ceremonies connect Jews with other Jews; the emphasis of the life cycle is to clarify what it is to be a Jew. In contrast, the narratives about African centered rites of passage imply that rites are a means by which one finds oneself. The rituals and ceremonies not only mark transition but are meant to develop personality and purpose.

14

Through the rites process initia*tes* will find their true selves; they are out there somewhere and it is through understanding their heritage, cultural rituals, and ceremonies that they will define themselves. However, there were common themes of continuity, linkage, understanding the given situation, self-consciousness, self-identity, and parental involvement. These narratives also suggest that whether an initiate is an African American or a Jew, no matter what he or she does, it is to be done as an African American or a Jew, respectively.

African Centered Rites of Passage

Culture is an integral part of rites of passage. Generally, culture has been defined as a system of techniques acquired and shared by members of a recognizable group, in order to generate acceptable solutions to problems (Ullman, 1965): the process of generating heritage. (See page 32) Specifically, the function of culture is to:

(1) Provide a lens of perception or cognitive frame work in which to view the world.
(2) Delineate standards of evaluation by which to measure worth or legitimacy, beauty, and truth.
(3) Define the conditions and means that motivate or stimulate a member (institutional or individual) of society and prescribe sanctions for disruptive digression.
(4) Define collective and individual identity, roles, and responsibilities.
(5) Provide a common language or means of communication.
(6) Provide the basis for social organization.
(7) Condition the mode of production.
(8) Delineate a process for perpetuation of the culture [rites of passage]. (adapted from Akoto, 1992, pp. 31–32)

15

Rites of passage are the means by which a society perpetuates its culture. However, when society is disrupted, as in the case of involuntary minorities, often formal rites of passage are abandoned or stripped away. To compensate, segments of a community, especially the youth, will either create their own rites or adopt the rites of others (Cohen, 1991). Under these circumstances, rites tend to convey distorted cultural wisdom, frames of reference and values. Though African Americans tend to have a style, a mode of operation, that is based on African concepts (Boykin, 1986; Patton, 1993), many of the rites and ceremonies in the African American community are not based on African heritage, values, and philosophies (Akoto, 1992; Ani, 1994; Asante, 1987; Benjamin, 1993; Somè, 1994; Wilson, 1993; Woodson, 1933/1990).

Public schools, debutante balls, beautilions, gang initiations, and incarceration are some examples of non–African centered rites of passage which have been adopted by the African American community (Hill, 1992; Majors & Billson, 1992; Perkins, 1986). Non–culturally centered rituals in the African American community, especially among the youth, often focus on physical manifestations rather than on spiritual/value representation. In terms of the rites of passage process, the emphasis is on the transition rather than the process (preparation through reincorporation) which justifies the transition. Take, for example, childbearing; once used as a marker for adulthood, certain values, commitment, and the ability to take care of the child were implied. However, the abandonment of African centered rites of passage has allowed childbearing to be disconnected. Consequently, many have confused the act of childbearing with the values that justified it as a marker of adulthood.

Another example is the coming-out ceremonies and balls which have replaced adulthood initiation among some segments of the African American community.

Though the intent of coming-out ceremonies is the same as that of African centered adult initiation rites, the contents are often different. Ceremonies that require waltzing and reward individuals for raising the most money tend not to convey African centered values. All too often such ceremonies imply that "cultured" individuals are those that have developed an appreciation for or mastery of European art forms and philosophies. Recently, many coming-out ceremonies have tried to include African cultural references by having participants wear kente cloth and the like. All this is superficial if the basic philosophies and values are disconnected from African heritage and ethos.

The quandary created is what Boykin (1986) describes as the need to negotiate between traditional African propensities and Euro-American cultural ethos. In Mike's narrative, he discusses a similar concept:

> Historically, if we look at the fact that whichever group dominated because of wars, because of colonialism, search anywhere around the globe, that particular ruling class forced conditions on the ones they overthrew to adopt their particular way of life. In doing that, we can forget that we are victims of colonialism, and we've adopted that colonialized lifestyle, not realizing that is not what we are. That is not what we were. . . . And I say that all the time: blacks in the United States have forgotten who they were before. We've been colonized and taken over, stripped, and put somewhere else, to the extent, now, that we believe that it was always like this. There was nothing else.

The rites of passage process is only significant relative to its cultural base (Hill, 1992; Perkins, 1986; van Gennep, 1908/1960; Warfield-Coppock, 1992, 1994). It is through these rituals and ceremonies that frames of reference, cultural lenses, and filters are constructed. Thus, culturally based rites of passage help create a philosophical context (place) in which one can critically examine and interpret the world (Afrik, 1993; Akoto, 1992; Ani, 1994; Shujaa, 1994; Warfield-Coppock, 1992, 1994; Wilson, 1993). Therefore, the rites of passage process in the African American community should (must) be African centered.

Asante (1987, p. 6) defines Afrocentricity (African centered) as the placing of African ideals at the center of any analysis that involves African culture and behavior. Karenga (1994, p. 36) provides a similar definition:

> Afrocentricity can be defined as a quality of thought and practice rooted in the cultural image and human interest of African people [and their descendants]. To be rooted in the cultural image of African people is to be anchored in the views and values of African people as well as in the practice which emanates from and gives rise to these views and values.

Both definitions imply that to be African centered is to construct and use frames of reference, cultural filters, and behaviors that are consistent with the philosophies and heritage of African cultures in order to advance the interest of people of African descent (Keto, 1991).

Boykin (1986) suggests that a traditional West African ethos is characterized by (1) Spirituality, (2) Harmony, (3) Movement, (4) Verve, (5) Affect, (6) Communalism, (7) Expressive Individualism, (8) Oral Tradition, and (9) Social Time Perspective. This is consistent with research by Ani (1994), Asante (1987), Karenga (1994), Maquet (1967/1972), and Patton (1993). In 1971 Steve Biko presented a paper at a conference in Natal South Africa that confirms the research of recent scholars:

> Obviously the African culture has had to sustain severe blows and may have been battered nearly out of shape by the belligerent cultures it collided with, yet in essence even today one can easily find the

fundamental aspects of the pure African culture in the present day African. . . . One of the most fundamental aspects of our culture is the importance we attach to Man. . . .a Man-centered society. . . .the capacity we have for talking to each other—not for the sake of arriving at a particular conclusion but merely to enjoy the communication for its own sake. . . .We regard our living together not as an unfortunate mishap warranting endless competition among us but as a deliberate act of God to make us a community of brothers and sisters jointly involved in the quest for a composite answer to the varied problems of life. . . . Any suffering we experienced was made much more real by song and rhythm. There is no doubt that the so called "Negro Spirituals" sung by black slaves in the States as they toiled under oppression were indicative of their African heritage. . . . African society had the village community as its basis. . . . This obviously was a requirement to suit the needs of a community-based and man-centered society.

Africans do not recognize any cleavage between the natural and supernatural. They experience a situation rather than face a problem. . . . More as a response of the total personality to the situation than the result of some mental exercise. . . . We thanked God through our ancestors before we drank beer, married, worked, etc. We would obviously find it artificial to create special occasions for worship. God was always in communication with us and therefore merited attention everywhere and anywhere. (Biko, 1978, pp. 41–45)

Reflective of the diversity on the African continent, there are many different forms of African centered rites of passage being practiced by African American churches, community groups, independent schools, and families (Afrik, 1993; Lewis, 1988; Warfield-Coppock, 1992, 1994). There are a number of value systems, such as Nguzo Saba, Ma'at, religious systems (Christianity, Islam, ancestral), and tribal traditions (Akan, Yoruba) through which the African centered rites of passage has been conveyed. However, at the foundation of African centered rites and ceremonies are the basic principles of spirituality, interdependence, cooperation, respect, reciprocity, intergenerational balance, understanding and developing purpose, cultural competence every person has a built-in capacity to succeed, and youths cannot effectively teach themselves to be adults (Hill, 1992, M.E.C.C.A., n.d.; Perkins, 1986; Warfield-Coppock, 1992, 1994).

The literature and the narratives suggest that the purpose of African centered rites of passage is to make conscious the development of self, which fosters (1) internal locus of control, (2) the ability to transform and interpret information, (3) historical continuity, (4) development of purpose, and (5) fictive kinship among community members (Afrik, 1993; Akoto, 1992; Fraser, 1994; Hare & Hare, 1985; Hill, 1992; M.E.C.C.A., n.d.; Perkins, 1986, Somè, 1994; Warfield-Coppock, 1992, 1994).

CHAPTER 2

SENSE OF SELF AND THE EDUCATIVE EXPERIENCE

Many scholars have researched various aspects of the self: self-esteem, self-appraisal, self-image, self-identity, as examples, and their impact on a student's academic performance (Akoto, 1992; Boykin, 1986; Durgans, 1992; Fordham, 1988, 1991; Gary & Booker, 1992; Gerardi, 1990; Goggins & Lindbeck, 1986; Harris, 1993; Irvine, 1991; Johnson, 1993; Lee, 1984; Lent, Brown & Larkin, 1986; Macias, 1989; McMillan & Reed, 1994; O'Callaghan & Bryant, 1990; Salaam, 1992; Shade, 1989; Shujaa, 1994; Sowa, Thomson, & Bennett, 1989; Spaights, Kenner, & Dixon, 1986; Stokes, 1994; Tracey & Sedlacek, 1987; Wambach, 1993; Young & Sowa, 1992). Some researchers have not found a significant correlation between self-esteem and academic achievement (Durgans, 1992; Johnson, 1993; Kohn, 1994; Spaights, Kenner, & Dixon, 1986). It should be noted that many studies examine relationships between specific factors. It is unlikely that any one factor contributes significantly to academic success. However, it is more likely that academic success is a function of a process (Garibaldi, 1992b). Consequently, many studies have defined the factors too narrowly. Often, academic success is defined as grade point average (GPA), and the self is reduced to such components as self-esteem, self-image and identity.

To define academic success as only GPA considers a single indication of education (knowledge attainment) and not the broad scope of education as suggested by Nyerere (1967), Freire (1970), Goldschmidt (1977), and Hale-Benson (1986). As pointed out by Boykin (1986) and Fordham (1988), African American students who employ passive coping skills such as selling out and racelessness often earn high GPAs; however, this is negative academic success. African American students using passive coping skills have abandoned or distorted African self-consciousness (Boykin, 1986; Fordham, 1988; Majors & Billson, 1992).

These students have accepted values and beliefs that produce a false sense of their African selves. Thus, they confuse the interests of an oppressive system with their own and mimic the efforts of the oppressor (Ani, 1994; Asante, 1987; Biko, 1978; Boykin, 1986; Du Bois, 1903/1965; Frazier, 1973; Freire, 1970; Hale-Benson, 1986; Harrell, 1979; Shujaa, 1994; Stampp, 1956; Woodson, 1933/1990; West, 1994). This phenomenon is often reinforced by teachers who assume that students who act like them are trying harder and are more motivated than students that do not (Spindler & Spindler, 1990). For these students an inverse relationship exists between African self-conscious and GPA, therefore statistically negating any correlation between African self consciousness and GPA.

For example, in a study of African American college students from the University of Notre Dame, Western Michigan University, and Wittenberg University, Durgans (1992) did not find a significant correlation between African self-consciousness and GPA (which he defined as academic success). However, he did find a significant positive correlation between African self-consciousness, higher academic level (freshman through senior), and involvement in campus and community organizations. If Durgans's definition of academic success included not only GPA (knowledge attainment) but also matriculation through university and community involvement (knowledge application), then the results would have shown a more significant positive correlation between African self-consciousness and academic success.

Academic success should include traditional measures such as grade point average, test scores, graduation rates, and decreased disciplinary actions and absences, however it is the application of the attained knowledge that determines whether academic success is positive or negative. Positive academic success signifies that the knowledge attained is used for the development and maintenance of a society/culture. Positive academic success also suggests that the values and beliefs that foster active participation in a society have been transmitted. In contrast, negative academic success signifies that the knowledge attained is not used for the development or maintenance of the society, or the values and beliefs transmitted do not encourage active participation by the student. An African American student must not only achieve a high grade point average but also find and fulfill a purpose in the African American community (Du Bois, 1903/1965; Fordham, 1988, 1991; Hale-Benson, 1986).

The other problem with most studies is the self. All too often the self is treated as a single-dimensional concept, as if one could draw conclusions about relationships between the self and other phenomena by measuring a single aspect such as self-esteem (Kohn, 1994). As the saying goes, ignorance is bliss. Especially for African Americans, positive self-esteem does not necessarily translate into authentic self-consciousness. Oppressive systems often reward those who abandon an authentic self for the interests of the system (Freire, 1970; Stampp, 1956). These rewards may be acceptance into particular social or academic circles, appointment to overseeing positions, or material compensation. Unfortunately, without a sense of self, one will confuse such rewards with a measure of self-worth. In this preencounter state (Cross, Parham, & Helms, 1991), unable to see past the veil (Du Bois, 1903/1965) of their oppression, many African Americans feel good about who and what they have become. I maintain that self-esteem (how one feels about one's self) and self-consciousness (understanding of one's self) are often related but are not synonymous, and also that self-consciousness has a greater impact on academic success than does feeling good about one's self.

The literature suggests that the self is a multidimensional concept. Many psychologists, including Erikson, Piaget, Freud, and Rogers, suggest that the self is made up of many components (Patterson, 1986; Shaffer, 1993). Rogers (1951) defined the configuration of self as being:

composed of such elements as the perceptions of one's characteristics and abilities; the percepts and concepts of self in relation to others and to the environment; the value qualities which are perceived as associated with experiences and objects; and goals and ideas which are perceived as having positive or negative valence. (pp. 136–137)

Akbar (1985) reiterated the complexity of the self in his work *The Community of Self*. Akbar discusses the interplay of various "members" of the self and the need for harmonious cooperation in order for one to endure (succeed) despite extreme opposition. *Sense of self* refers to one's awareness (consciousness) of these interactions and their effects.

Research that examines the relationships between self and academic success should consider knowledge application and attainment as well as using a holistic approach to the self.

The need for a sense of self in education

Arguments have been made for the need for the self in education. In 1933, Carter G. Woodson provided a thorough explanation of the absence of the African (Negro) self in American educational systems in the classic *The Mis-Education of the Negro* (1933/1990). He pointed out that traditional education did not consider African Americans except to condemn or pity them. Nor did the curriculum acknowledge the origins of the contributions of Africans or the contributions themselves:

> . . . the Negro, according to this point of view, was an exception to the natural plan of things, and he had no such mission as that of an outstanding contribution to culture. The status of the Negro, then, was just fixed as that of an inferior (p. 22).

Woodson suggested that the "mis-education" of African Americans has led to the enslaving of their minds, which is evident by their actions. Woodson suggested that

24

mis-educated African Americans act out of the interest and purpose of others, which has led to economic, social, and intellectual stagnation in the African American community.

Though Woodson examined the specifics of the African American experience with traditional education, philosopher John Dewey discussed it in more general terms and reached many of the same conclusions. Dewey, in *Experience and Education* (1938/1963), suggested that by the principle of experiential continuum, every experience takes something from those experiences which have gone before and modifies in some way, the quality of those experiences which come after; this is a criterion to discriminate between educative and mis-educative experiences. Educative experiences empower students to exercise freedom and move toward fulfillment of their purpose, while mis-educative experiences are disconnected and do not move students toward empowerment and fulfillment. Dewey also argued that disconnected experiences make self-control (internal locus) impossible. He suggested that a person with only such disconnected experiences would reach a point of insanity; the students are robbed of their ability to cope with their life circumstances successfully.

Dewey clearly saw the need for self in order to make an experience educative. If there is no self, there is no formation of self-purpose, nor is there intelligence: the means by which a student strategizes to execute a purpose. When the self is removed from an experience (schooling), the result is a slave: one who executes the purposes of another (Dewey, 1938/1963, p. 67).

In *The Pedagogy of the Oppressed*, Paulo Freire (1970) discussed schooling for the oppressed. Though Freire often described issues in Brazil, conceptually his conclusion supports the arguments made by Woodson and Dewey: meaningful education must consider and empower the student. Freire suggested that the projection of absolute ignorance onto others is a characteristic of the ideology of oppression.

In education, this characteristic is manifested in what Freire described as a "banking" concept:

> Education thus becomes an act of depositing, in which the students are the depositories and the teacher is the depositor. . . . The more students work at storing the deposits entrusted to them, the less they develop the critical consciousness which would result from their intervention in the world as transformers of that world. . . . There are innumerable well-intentioned bank-clerk teachers who do not realize that they are serving only to dehumanize. . . . The banking concept of education, . . . attempts to control thing and action, leads women and men to adjust to the world, and inhibits their creative power. (pp. 53–58)

Freire argued that education for the oppressed must develop critical thinking and their ability to transform their world. Therefore, it is necessary that the pedagogy be derived from praxis, the reflection and action of the oppressed. This educative process will result in the emergence of self consciousness (understanding more clearly one's purpose and self-identity), so that one can more wisely build the future. According to Freire, striving for self-consciousness is the starting point for the educational process.

Hale-Benson (1986) develops this argument further. She suggests that schooling developed under a system of oppression tends to aid in cultural repression of the oppressed and to create a rationale for oppression. Thus, the oppressed are taught to synthesize the experiences and memorize the conclusions of another people: the oppressor. African Americans are inclined to confuse their interests with those of their oppressor (Stampp, 1956). Therefore, African Americans tend to accept the mainstream's definitions of the problems that society has caused and the solutions it deems acceptable. Hale-Benson proposes "Black Education" as a solution for African American students.

According to Hale-Benson, the goal of Black Education is to consistently make students conscious of struggle and commitment. It must instill a revolutionary sense of identity. African American students must develop an alternative frame of reference, positive self-concepts, an African identity, and commitment to their community, which will allow students to be conscious of (1) who they are, (2) who the enemy is, (3) what the enemy is doing to them, (4) what to struggle for, and (5) what form the struggle must take.

Woodson, Dewey, Freire, and Hale-Benson reflect philosophically the argument for progressive education, which by definition must consider the student's sense of self. Their argument also assumes that there is a self to consider. The student must have some sense of continuity and purpose for an experience to be educative. Thus, these aspects of self must be at some stage of development before the experience takes place (Gowin, 1981). Along with the philosophical arguments, other researchers have developed many behavioral and learning process models, many of which at least imply a sense of self. Consider Shade's (1989) Information Processing Model:

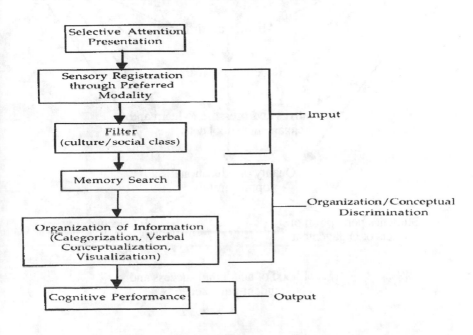

In Shade's (1989) discussion of the African American cognitive pattern, she suggests that African Americans generally have a "preferred" process of obtaining knowledge, and that this difference manifests itself through worldview. Shade also points out that individuals are taught to interpret the world; specifically, African American culture trains its children how to learn. Though the primary focus of Shade (1989) is to identify a unique cognitive pattern for African Americans, she strongly implies that cognitive performance is a function of the self (as defined by Rogers, 1951), with filters and reference points provided by culture.

Montgomery et al. (1993) give a conceptual framework of youth development and educational performance:

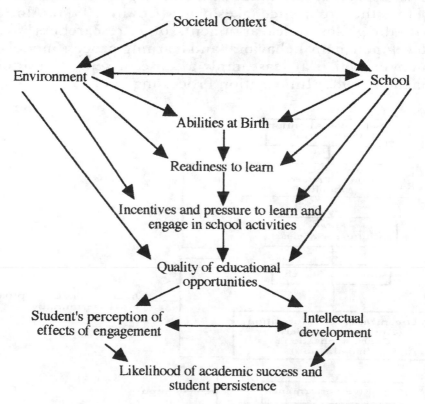

The bases of this model are the environment, school-based resources, and the decision of the student to invest in academic achievement. According to Montgomery et al., the interactions between these factors are the determinants of the student's "readiness to learn." By using terms like "student perception," Montgomery et al. indicate a recognition of a sense of self by the student. They also suggest that not all factors must be optimal in order to foster academic success. Developing a positive sense of self may compensate for societal and teacher perceptions.

Irvine (1991) gives a process model for black student achievement:

A Process Model for Black Student Achievement

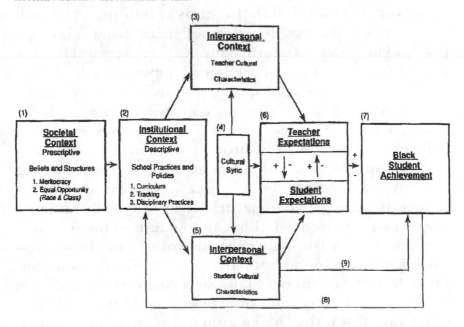

Irvine's model illustrates some of the factors significant for black student achievement. She argues that black students are at greater risk of failure because of their race, social class, and culture. However, she is careful to note that not all black students are equally at risk. She suggests that a major contributor to underachievement and the lack of motivation of African American students is their acceptance of American mainstream society's view that African Americans are unlikely to succeed. Irvine focuses on strategies aimed at teachers, administration, and parents. However, what she strongly implies is the need to reshape African American students' view of themselves.

In each of these models there is a recognition that a sense of self must be brought to the experience. The experience in and of itself does not create significant meaning; rather, the student must "make meaning" (Gowin, 1981). When a person's sense of self has been defined beyond a set of conditions, those circumstances become a means to an end, even if they are meant to be hostile or oppressive (Frankl, 1962). In terms of traditional schooling, a student that is able to identify educative (empowering) and mis-educative (enslaving) experiences will be able to use those experiences for self-development (Gowin, 1981).

For example, when I was nine years old, I spent three months visiting seven African countries: Senegal, Ivory Coast, Benin, Nigeria, Tanzania, Kenya, and Ethiopia. This experience had a profound influence on my education. Specifically, when teachers or the media would present information about Africa or African people, it tended to be negative in nature. This often contradicted what I had experienced. I began to question the teachers and the motives for their presentations. I not only questioned information about Africa and African people but asked how Columbus could discover America if there were people already here, and how Lewis and Clark could discover the West if they had a guide. I came to two conclusions: (1) people misrepresent the truth because they are ignorant or do not want to face the effects of the truth; and (2) the information presented in school and the media was a reflection of interpretations, not absolutes. So I learned that a course labeled World History may in fact be about the development of Europe; that what is labeled classical music is really European classical music; and that tests given in these subjects reflect these same perceptions.

This process is described by Karenga (1995) as "place making":

> We have to be able to arise above our original circumstance, create place out of no place, and way out of no way, and something out of what looks originally like nothing. Let's look at the pre-creation and see if we can imitate God in that way. . . . Be a place-maker. Take the models in history that made a place. Listen to that. The place made by the Creator is place making because He made place out of no place. There was no place for Him; He made place. He didn't whine about the darkness. . . .[He] perceived infinity and projected it out and differentiated himself [from it]. . . . Place making. Frederick Douglass, in his autobiography of slavery, said that there is no place for blacks to learn to read and write, so he creates a place. Nat Turner; place-maker. There's no place for a black man in the halls of slavery to take off his chains and put them around his oppressor's neck. Nat Turner place-makes. He don't ask for a key, he kicks the door in. Malcolm X; place making. He didn't wait for some outside force to tell him what man is. . . . He makes a place for himself. . . . That was his criteria for manhood, waking up. Place-make you black man. You'll see how beautiful your life is.

The place one makes is the place in which one makes meaning, defines oneself, finds purpose, and interacts with the world. Frame of reference, self-consciousness, lenses, and sense of self all refer in part or in total to the place Karenga has suggested be made. This parallels Freire's (1970) argument for praxis, reflection, and action. Having a sense of self that has been developed outside a situation allows for the critical examination of conditions with different values, expectations, and perceptions, thus creating a new situation.

Consider the following model of transformation[2]:

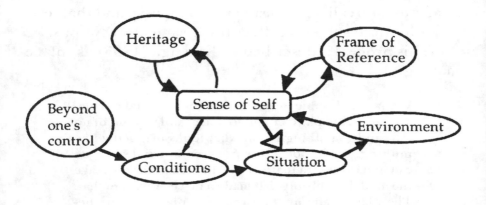

---

[2] *Frame of reference/Worldview* The philosophical conceptual framework for seeing reality and understanding order. This includes an individual's concept of the relationships between self, nature, and society.

Heritage refers to the set of techniques, strategies, and traditions (collective wisdom) developed to solve problems of existence, which are based upon the contributions of ancestors, elders, and those in the current generation. Heritage, as it is defined here, is not a static heirloom simply passed from one generation to the next, but the dynamic interaction of antiquity and the present. This definition also implies the collective and specific nature of heritage. There is a common heritage shared by a group of people. However, there are specific traits more prevalent within certain subgroups, such as a family.

Conditions are the existing circumstances, which may have been (1) beyond the control of the individual, (2) created or influenced by individual, or (3) a combination of (1) and (2).

Situation is one's status in regard to conditions. However, consider the following: Status is contingent upon one's evaluation of the circumstances. Evaluation is a function of the self (Rogers, 1951). Thus, for the purpose of this study, situation is defined as the manifestation of the self through the application of values and ethos on a particular set of conditions.

Environment is the natural, social, and cultural situations that affect development of the self.

In terms of education, there are a number of conditions over which a student has little to no control. Most obvious are the historical information and absolute facts such as: There are fifty states in the United States of America, and the value statement $2 + 2 = 4$. The history of the Eurocentric racist hegemony prevalent in the American school system and the corresponding effects on curriculum, teachers' expectations, and funding practices are other conditions students have little to no control over. Another example is the parents' socioeconomic status and the related ramifications. However, not all conditions are beyond the control of the student. Each student contributes something to the set of circumstances with which every other student must contend, even if it is just the student-teacher ratio.

Whatever the influences that affect the conditions, students must evaluate them, thus creating the situation. Shade's (1989) Information Process Model is an excellent illustration of the evaluation process. The situations become a part of the student's environment, which affects the development of self. As a sense of self develops, it will influence/modify the frame of reference and contribute to heritage. This process transforms schooling into education only if (1) the connections to heritage have been made, and (2) the development of worldview has been influenced by heritage. If not, the values inherent in the conditions will be transmitted unchecked and unexamined into the environment, thus, creating an environment that may not encourage connections and contributions to heritage therefore hindering access to the cultural wisdom necessary for the development of a healthy frame of reference and sense of self.

The literature suggests that (1) the self is not an isolated entity but an interrelation of abilities, values, (fictive) kinship, environment, and cultural heritage; (2) these variables (sense of self) are important factors in determining one's academic performance; (3) one must possess the ability to transform and reinterpret information if not one can only act out the purposes of others and (4) educative experiences foster the development of self. Therefore, it is necessary for African Americans to develop a sense of self based on African centered heritage, culture, and philosophies: an authentic self. If not, there will be little change in the academic conditions of our students. An educative experience requires a connection between the student, cultural heritage, and community (Dewey, 1938/1963). Unfortunately, this does not typically happen in the American school system.

CHAPTER 3

SCHOOLING AFRICAN AMERICANS

Historical Overview of American Assumptions and Beliefs:

For 246 (1619–1865) of the 377 (1619–1996) years (65.25%), the prevailing status or definition of African people by American society was one of property. By the Revolutionary War, the legal status of the African slave was clearly defined in the courts of all the colonies. Africans were either chattel or real property (Williams, 1886/1968). School systems were instituted to prepare Africans for their role in society.

Seasoning was a learning process that taught Yoruba, Mandingo, Hausa, Ibo, and others to be slaves. To ensure the internalization of slave status, seasoning was often characterized by brutal physical abuse, separation from family and tribe members, forbidding the practice of one's culture (language, religion, and other social norms), harsh living conditions, renaming (defining), and cognitive development determined by others (Pinkney, 1975; Stampp, 1956). Though seasoning would not be considered a formal educational process, there were laws or slave codes that served as guidelines on what a slave could be taught and to limit slaves' participation in society. In *Narrative of the Life of Frederick Douglass,* Douglass (1945/1968) gives vivid examples of seasoning. Probably one of the better known examples dramatized was in the *Roots* miniseries, where Kunta Kente was whipped until he would answer, "My name is Toby." The intended outcome of the seasoning process is to make bondage a habit by making yielding to oppression the only practical choice (Stampp, 1956).

According to Stampp (1956), control was best institutionalized when slave masters:

1. established and maintained strict discipline. . . It greatly impairs the happiness of a negro, to cultivate an insubordinate temper.

2. implanted in the [slaves] a consciousness of personal inferiority. They had to know and keep their places, to feel the difference between master and slave, to understand that bondage was their natural status.
3. trained [school] slaves to be awed with a sense of their master's enormous power. The only principle upon which slavery could be maintained was the power of fear.
4. persuaded the [slaves] to take an interest in the master's enterprise and to accept his standards of good conduct [values]. . . . The master should make it his business to show his slaves that the advancement of his individual interest is at the same time an advancement of theirs. Once they feel this, it will require but little compulsion to make them act as it becomes them.
5. impressed Negroes with their helplessness, to create in them a perfect habit of dependence on their masters. Many believed it was dangerous to teach slaves to be skilled artisans in the towns, because they tended to become self-reliant . . . got a habit of roaming and taking care of themselves . . . it produces in the slave an unwillingness to return to the regular life and domestic control of the master. (pp. 144–147)

Though formal educational systems for Africans often started as efforts to convert them to Christianity, the basic values and assumptions taught in the informal systems were perpetuated. French Catholics in Louisiana were among the earliest group to begin providing instruction to African slaves in the early 1600s. A French *code noir*, a system of laws for black people, made it incumbent upon masters to educate slaves (Estelh, 1994). However, given the slave status of the Africans, the schooling they received from the masters prepared them to be slaves. Like the French slave owners, many of the missionaries believed in the humanity of the Africans but did not view them as equals. In 1701 the Church of England organized the Society for Gospel in Foreign Parts to convert African slaves to Christianity and provide them an education (Estelh, 1994). As early as 1667, the Virginia colonial legislature passed a law that would encourage slave owners to convert their slaves to Christianity without fear that the newly baptized Christian brother would therefore cease to be a slave. These laws of the 1660s paved the way for the statutes passed by the Virginia legislature in 1670 that enslaved all blacks coming to the colony. All Africans were to be slaves for life (Pinkney, 1975; Toppin, 1971). So, regardless of the socialization or education instituted, formal or informal, it was designed to prepare Africans to be slaves in the social structure.

Abolitionists played an important part in the creation of schools for free Africans. However, many abolitionists did not believe in the equality of the African culture with white culture (Filler, 1960). On September 28, 1858, Abraham Lincoln stated in a campaign speech:

> I am not, nor have I ever been in favor of bringing about in any way, the social and political equality of the white and black races. That I am not nor ever been in favor of making voters or jurors of Negroes, nor of qualifying them to hold office, nor to intermarry with white people. And I will say in addition to this, that there is a difference between the white and black races, which I believe will forever forbid the two races living together on terms of social and political equality. And inasmuch as they cannot so live, while they do remain together, there must be the position of superior and inferior, and I as much as any man I am in favor of having the superior position assigned to the white race (from Steinfield, 1972).

President Abraham Lincoln saw no "place for Negroes in the United States." He had hoped to send Africans back to Africa, Haiti, or to a colony in Central America (*Current*, 1958). President Abraham Lincoln stated in a letter:

> If I could save the Union without freeing the slaves, I
> would do it; if I could save it by freeing all the slaves, I
> would do it; and if I could save it by freeing some and
> leaving others alone, I would also do that. What I do
> about slavery and the colored race, I do because I be-
> lieve it helps save the Union.

Even the ending of slavery was not done for the benefit of African people and did little to change the status of Africans; "with emancipation the Negro lost nothing, but his chains" (Stampp, 1956, p. 430).

During Reconstruction, Africans were granted citizenship and the right to vote. However, Congress was still at odds about the African's place in America. Many in the federal government demanded that the South should remain a white man's country, while others stated that the government was a government of all men and that the goal of reconstruction was to give African Americans equity before the law (Goode, 1969; Filler, 1960).

Organizations such as the Ku Klux Klan, Knights of the White Camellia, Knights of the White Rose, Pale Faces, Red Jacks, Knights of the Black Cross, White Brotherhood, and Constitutional Guards were formed because African Americans and their white allies confused freedom with equality (Loh, 1994).

The Reconstruction period was short–lived because of a compromise between Congress and the southern states in 1877 (Goode, 1969). With the end of Reconstruction, southern legislature passed Jim Crow laws. These laws, similar to the slave codes, were designed to limit and define the status of African Americans.

Since Reconstruction, there have been two significant Supreme Court rulings which reflect and shape attitudes toward educating African Americans: (1) *Plessy* v. *Ferguson* in 1896 and (2) *Brown* v. *Board of Education of Topeka* in

1954. *Plessy* v. *Ferguson* ruled "separate but equal." This decision would allow for separate educational systems to continue, in theory, providing everything in one system that would be provided in the other. This was a compromise between the laws that define African Americans as full citizens "equal under the law" and the history of segregation. Though the Supreme Court called for separate but equal, the application was separate and unequal. Generally, schools and districts that were predominately populated by African Americans would receive less money and outdated or inadequate materials, thus providing an inferior and unequal educational system (Toppin, 1971).

The Supreme Court decision in the case of *Brown* v. *Board of Education of Topeka* in 1954 ended legal segregation. This decision was pivotal in providing access to equal facilities and in theory equal educational opportunities. Lawyers argued that an all African American class would be inferior to an all white class regardless of the money spent. The Supreme Court agreed:

> In these days, it is doubtful that any child may reasonably be expected to succeed in life if he is denied the opportunity of an education. Such an opportunity . . . must be made available to all on equal terms.

> We come to the question presented: Does segregation of the children in public schools solely on the basis of race, even though the physical facilities and other "tangible" factors may be equal, deprive the children of the minority group of the equal educational opportunities? We believe that it does. . . . To separate them from others of similar age and qualifications solely because of their race generates a feeling of inferiority as to their status in the community that may affect their hearts and minds in a way unlikely ever to be undone. . . .

> We conclude that in the field of public education the doctrine of "separate but equal" has no place. Separate educational facilities are inherently unequal.

In fact, the argument that segregated classes would inherently mean an inferior education for African American children was based on the perceived inferiority of African Americans. The Court's decision did little to redefine the perceived inferior status of African Americans in the mainstream educational system (Afrik, 1993). What it did do was to perpetuate the idea of the white man's burden.

In a 1899 poem, "The White Man's Burden," Rudyard Kipling describes the "burden" as the responsibility of the white man to "look after" the affairs of the darker races. In particular, the Anglo-Saxons of Britain and America should accept their "Christian" duty to help the poor colored masses to find a better way (Knowles & Prewitt, 1969; Maquet, 1967/1972). This attitude has led to the general characterization of people of African descent as disadvantaged, culturally deprived, dysfunctional, at risk, permanent underclass, and other nomenclature derived from a deficiency analysis. The phenomenon of viewing others as deficient based on one's own perceived superiority is not unique to the dynamics between mainstream America and African people. It is characteristic of oppressive systems to project ignorance onto the oppressed. Their so-called ignorance is often perceived as pathology resulting from their rejection of a "healthy" society (Freire, 1970). As a result, educational systems are designed to incorporate the oppressed into the "healthy" society. The purpose of such institutionalized manipulation is to maintain the status quo. As Carter G. Woodson (1933/1990) suggested:

> If you can control a man's thinking you do not have to worry about his action. When you determine what a man shall think you do not have to concern yourself with what he will do. If you make a man feel that he is inferior, you do not have to compel him to accept an inferior status, for he will seek it himself. (p. 84)

School systems have been among the primary agents in perpetuating the Eurocentric hegemony[3] in the United States. Subsequently, not only have African Americans developed a false sense of self and white European male Protestant supremacy, so has mainstream society.

Academic Implications of Mainstream's Assumptions and Values

American society has defined Africans as inferior and deficient, with no valid culture, value system, worldview, or intellectual tradition (Bond, 1966). Thus the schooling systems instituted were designed either to prepare people of African descent to fulfill inferior roles or to fix their deficiencies; note, schooling not education. *Schooling* can be characterized as monitored rote memorization where the information designed to perpetuate existing social structures is to be accepted as universal and true without critical examination or consideration for the unique genius (potential) of the student (Afrik, 1993; Ani, 1994; Asante, 1987; Biko, 1978; Hale-Benson, 1986; Shujaa, 1994). Therefore when studying academic indicators, e.g. standardized test scores or grade point average, one should understand that it may reflect more than just knowledge (or the lack of knowledge) and attainment. As Sowell (1986) stated:

[3.] *Hegemony*: the organized assemblage of beliefs and practices wielded by ruling groups (Marsh & Willis, 1995, p. 100); a self-reinforcing phenomenon that aids and abets the continuation of "things" as they are (Boykin, 1986, p. 70), typically perpetuated without critical examination. For example, the contributions of African people are not widely taught in American schools; therefore these contributions are not known. Thus, they cannot be taught. As the proverb says: You cannot teach what you do not know, You cannot lead where you will not go.

41

> Tests are not unfair. Life is unfair, and tests measure
> the results. Tests are not meant to predict what would
> happen in a vacuum, but what will happen in the real
> world. (p. 5)

Present national statistics reveal that African American students as a group are not performing as well academically as other groups. African American students lead in too many of the wrong statistics. The literature suggests that low academic performance by African Americans is not a new phenomenon. Researchers have examined the academic performance of African Americans for many years. African American students as a group are outperformed on IQ and other standardized tests, high school drop-out rates, and college graduation rates.

Some researchers have tried to explain this phenomenon as a biological function, i.e., blacks are genetically less intelligent than whites, too violent, or too "hyper" to learn (Powell, 1992). These researchers offer solutions such as lower expectations and chemical treatments. Though the research and conclusions of many of these scholars are suspect, they agree with the general consensus, the unexamined realities of an Eurocentric hegemony, which allows the research to resonate with a certain trueness.

In contrast, there is a much wider body of scholarly work that has researched the impact of social factors on academic performance. As previously noted, many researchers used a deficiency analysis for African Americans, and their solutions tend to suggest a need for compensation programs designed to align African American student learning styles and values with the mainstream. There are, however, an increasing number of scholars focusing on the effects of teaching styles, curriculum, and societal expectations on academic success.

Ogbu's research (1974, 1986, 1991) has focused on the low academic performance of subordinate/castelike/involuntary minorities. Much of Ogbu's discussion describes the consequences of the American caste system in terms of low IQ scores and school performance. Ogbu's research shows that immigrant minorities, those groups who became a part of a society voluntarily, tend to have better academic performance than involuntary minorities, those groups who were made a part of a society through slavery, conquest, or colonization. Ogbu (1991) suggests there are differences in the cultural models used by immigrant and involuntary minorities:

> The more academically successful minorities differ from the less academically successful minorities in the type of cultural model that guides them, that is, in the type of understanding they have of the workings of the larger society and of their place as minorities in that working order. (p. 8)

The differences are functions of the initial terms of incorporation into the society and the patterns of adaptive responses to subsequent discriminatory treatment by members of the dominant group. Also, those groups that experience greater academic success tend to have a positive frame of reference and an optimistic view of their future, along with a positive sense of cultural identity. This allows a basis from which they can determine what they like and dislike about American mainstream culture.

Even those African American students who enroll in college tend not to perform as well as their white counterparts. African American students at predominately white colleges fare the worst. One continuing explanation has been the alleged genetic inferiority of African Americans, recently expressed by the president of Rutgers University (Russakoff, 1995). However, more careful analyses have been provided.

Fleming (1991) compared and contrasted students at historically black colleges and universities (HBCUs) and predominately white colleges. Fleming suggests that

HBCUs provide an atmosphere that allows opportunities for friendship, participation in campus life, and feeling some sense of progress and success in their academic pursuits. Fleming points out these ingredients parallel the basis of motivation and humanistic theory. Fleming also suggests there is a connection between intellectual and social issues, and that academic performance may equal or exceed the sum of intellectual and social adjustment. Using Erikson as a basis, Fleming states,

> there is a critical interaction between the factors that individuals bring to the educational setting and the opportunities for change within that setting. (p. 22)

Hale-Benson (1986) discusses the differences between and the origins of African American and European American learning styles. She states:

> One reason for the high level of failure rates of some cultural minorities is the mismatch between the school culture and the social, cultural, and experiential background of minority students. (p. 103)

Hale-Benson's argument is supported by the research of Boykin (1986) and Irvine (1991). The cultural relationship between traditional schooling and the student is described as cultural synchronization by Irvine. Given cultural synchronization as the cause of the problem, if the school curriculum and environment are changed to be more synchronized with the particular learning styles and cultural background of the students, then an improvement in the school performance of African American and other cultural minority students in public schools will occur (Boykin, 1986; Fleming, 1991; Hale-Benson, 1986; Irvine, 1991; Patton, 1993). This would require a basic philosophical change in public education. However, considering who is perpetuating the Eurocentric hegemony, this is unlikely.

Many teachers/professors do not maliciously perpetuate racist beliefs and assumptions about African American students. McClendon (1995) states:

> Some of the problems related to the ineffective and poor schooling of African American children is surely related to who is currently teaching them, and it may not be a matter of blatant racism but rather a matter of teachers not being able to relate to the "otherness" of the students. Who is teaching our children?

A national profile of teachers by the American Association of Colleges for Teacher Education reveals some interesting information about who is teaching, who will be teaching, and who is teaching future teachers.

Who is teaching?

The typical teacher is a white female about forty years old, a married mother of two, works in a suburban elementary school, and is not politically active.

Who will be teaching?

National profile of education majors: about 76% are female, 91% of whom are white. Less than 7% are minorities. The typical college student majoring in education is a white female from a small town or suburban community. She tends to go to a college less than 100 miles from home and intends to return home to work. She views teaching as fulfilling a vocational need to work. She wants to teach middle-income children of average intelligence, in traditionally organized schools.

Who is teaching the teachers?

Profile of college faculty in education: about 70% white males; 91% white overall. Typically conformist with utilitarian views of knowledge; many from a lower-middle-class background.

One can conclude from these data that it is doubtful that systemic change will occur anytime soon. Also, given the teacher profile and the history of the educational system for African Americans in the United States, it is unwise to expect or want public schools to be the primary enculturation influence. The literature strongly suggests that academic indicators may reflect not knowledge attainment but how well a student is coping with society.

Coping Skills

Coping skills are the strategies employed by students to negotiate the dynamics between the cultural reference of the educational system and the self. Boykin (1986) suggests that in order to properly understand the interactions between the student and the educational system, one must consider four distinct planes: (1) what students do or do not do; 2) what they can or cannot do; (3) what they will or will not do; and (4) what they should or should not do.

For students with a high degree of cultural synchronization with the educational system, their academic performance (what they do) is based largely on what they can, will, and should do. Boykin (1986) states:

> In a culturally homogeneous population, what children actually do in an academic setting is based on what they can and will do, and what they understand that they should do. Similarly, what they don't do follows what they should not, will not, and cannot do. . . . Moreover, what the children themselves believe they should do is likely to be consistent with what their teachers believe: there is a congruence of value and belief. (pp. 76-77)

However, these assumptions for students who have a different cultural reference and experience an educational system that is hostile to their well-being would be inappropriate. The literature reveals a number of strategies used by African American students in order to cope with the lack of congruency in values, beliefs, and expectations between them and the educational system. These coping skills can be thought of in terms of two categories or varying frames of reference based on the oppressor and African self consciousness.

There has been a focus on coping skills that reflect a frame of reference which identifies with the oppressor. In this mode of thinking, African American students do not seriously consider possibilities other than existing. Boykin (1986) describes this type of thinking as "passive coping strategies."

Selling out, Uncle Tomming, acting white, and *punking out* all refer to an often-used strategy of African American students to win favor and success by enduring oppression as though it did not exist, and by abandoning their African integrity, styles, and consciousness. These students often find this strategy to be an effective way to gain academic success. They have become what the values of the school system would make of them, nonthreatening to the status quo (Fordham, 1988; Freire, 1970; Woodson, 1933/1990). Teachers often assume that students that act like them try harder and are more motivated, and reward the students accordingly (Spindler & Spindler, 1990). Unfortunately, this causes the illusion that academic prowess is a function of whiteness.

Racelessness is another effective strategy to gain academic success. Students that use this strategy believe their success depends on their abilities and/or how comfortable the mainstream feels with them (Fordham, 1988). Understanding that they cannot fully assimilate into being White and that being Black is detrimental, these students try to be un-Black. Naturally, their perception of what is Black is based on the negative perceptions of the mainstream. Here again the idea that success is a function of an African American student's ability to be un-African or un-Black is falsely reinforced.

Another strategy used by African American students is to beat them at their own game in an effort to get their fair share of the American pie (Boykin, 1986). Here again the assumption is that there is only one game to be played. The problem with the axiom, "As Blacks, we have to play the game twice as well as they do," is that as long as African Americans play the game, the outcome will be whatever the game produces, just twice as quick (Dewey, 1938/1963). Many times this leads to a crabs-in-the-bucket phenomenon.

Passive strategies tend to lead to an educated populace that is uncommitted to, unconcerned about, or ineffective in the uplift (development and maintenance) of the African American community. This has been a concern for a number of years. From before David Walker's appeal in 1830 to the present, many scholars and leaders have expressed a concern about *The Souls of Black Folk* (Du Bois, 1903/1965), "The Failure of the Negro Intellectual" (Frazier, 1973), and "The Dilemma of the Black Intellectual" (West, 1994). In other words, they worried about the ability of the educated African American to be relevant to the African American community.

Other forms of passive coping skills include hopelessness and oppositional culture. These tend not to produce academic success. African American students that have lost hope in education believe that society is too large to overcome and accept their defined lot in life. Education becomes pointless to one's ability to change one's situation. Their "locus of control" is external and perceived to be beyond their powers of manipulation (Goggins & Lindbeck, 1986).

On the other hand, increasing numbers of African American students are employing an oppositional culture strategy, which is falsely perceived as taking control (Dewey, 1938/1968). If people are in direct opposition to something, their first reference point is that "something." In order to be anti-white, students' first frame of reference is white, and they will construct a sense of self based on what is perceived to be white. For example, if education is something that white people do, then black people don't do it (Majors & Billson, 1992; Ogbu, 1991). This is dangerous because (1) it does not consider the commonalities of humanity; one constructs a sense of self that is not complete; (2) African American culture is only considered in its relation to the mainstream; by determining what is mainstream one can control what it is be to African American; and (3) it justifies the concept of a pathological existence for African Americans. African American students using passive coping skills have allowed the oppressor to define them and their situation. These students' usefulness to the African American community has to be seriously questioned.

Those students that maintain or develop frames of reference that are not based on the definitions and perceptions of the oppressor are said to have proactive coping skills. This mode of thinking does not deny the existence and the effects of oppression, nor do these students define themselves in relation to the oppressor. Rather, they recognize oppression as an obstacle to their fulfillment of self. Boykin (1986) describes one of the proactive coping skills as *dissembling*. Here, students conceal their true feelings and provide a pretense to the oppressive society, while performing subversive acts against the oppressor.

Students who adopt a distinct value system are best prepared to resist oppression (Durgans, 1992; Frankl, 1962; Harrell, 1979; Karenga, 1994, 1995). Ability to successfully endure oppressive and hostile environments increases when one's sense of self reflects one's cultural heritage and philosophies and provides historical continuity. A self-consciousness developed regardless of, not in response to or in spite of, oppression tends to have an insulating effect.

Research by Fordham (1991) supports this argument. Fordham suggests that traditional practices of "peer-proofing or protecting" high-achieving African American students have been largely unsuccessful due in part to the removal of these students from their peers, thus breaking fictive kinship (extended family) bonds. Fordham suggests that fictive kinship bonds are an important part of fitting into the African American community (Asante, 1987; Biko, 1978; Patton, 1993). When these bonds are broken, the high-achieving students become misfits in the African American community, at the same time not fitting into the dominant culture. In an earlier study, Fordham (1988) found that these students tended to adopt a racelessness coping skill.

Fordham's solution is to employ peer-proofing that is based on self-realization through service to the group. An example is the Professional Development Program (PDP) at the University of California, Berkeley. Many of the African American students were failing the math and science courses prerequisite for natural sciences careers. Some were high achievers at their former schools and many had family support and other factors associated with academic success. It was concluded that a hostile environment—the university; the lack of a supportive, academically focused peer group; and an unwillingness on the part of the students to seek help—contributed to the failure of the African American students. PDP was developed as an honors program that focuses on the strengths of the students and their willingness to collaborate with each other. The PDP has proven to be very successful. These students are now outperforming their fellow classmates. Fordham's findings are not surprising. Similar peer mentorship programs have had positive effects in many universities. These programs often incorporate culturally specific values and motifs.

There is a connection between social and intellectual aspects of a student. To reiterate, how African American students perform academically reflects their understanding of what they can, should, and will do (Boykin, 1986). Coping skills may reflect conscious choices or unconscious reactions. However, be they conscious or unconscious, the type of coping skill employed is based on a frame of reference and a sense of self.

For oppressed people, education must develop critical thinking, self-awareness, and purpose, even if in a hostile school system. Learning must be coupled with purpose (Dewey, 1938/1963; Du Bois, 1903/1965; Frankl, 1962; Freire, 1970; Hale-Benson, 1986), and purpose must be defined and rooted in the cultural heritage. This can be accomplished given a proper frame of reference that allows students to define themselves within a system, and not by a system (Butchart, 1994; Freire, 1970).

CHAPTER 4

ACADEMIC IMPLICATIONS OF AFRICAN CENTERED RITES OF PASSAGE

Kent State University Academic STARS.

The Academic STARS (Students Achieving and Reaching Success) at Kent State University is a program for new freshman designed to:

- recruit, retain, and graduate African American students
- help African American students make the transition from high school to the university
- provide each student with the necessary academic and life skills, such as self-discipline and determination, for a successful undergraduate experience

Any African American freshman who attended an Ohio high school and is admitted to Kent State University is eligible to participate in Academic STARS. A holistic approach to learning rooted in the African American experience is the basic philosophy of Academic STARS. From 1990 to 1994, the methods used were derived from various theories and strategies associated with learning styles, self-esteem, community education, community building, and culture. However, in 1995 the new class of Academic STARS went through African centered rites of passage. Though much of the material was the same, it was present in the rites of passage context.

Students were initiated into the university through an African centered rites of passage. The African American faculty and staff serve as mentors and elders, thus creating the village necessary for rites. Also, there is a rite of passage called the Karamu Ya Wahitimu for all African American students (undergraduate and graduate) who receive a degree.

In an interview with Michelle and Shana, the director and assistant director of the Office of Cultural Diversity, both stated that there is something "unique" about this group. Consistent with themes that emerged in the narratives of Mike and Donna, Michelle and Shana discussed developing community (fictive kinship), historical continuity, respect for self and others (peers and elders), development of purpose, increased confidence and maturity, parental involvement, and understanding one's responsibilities to the African American community.

Shana asserted: "It was like they went into a cocoon and emerged a different group of people; they're not the same group of kids we started out with. . . This group of students is not like any other that we've had."

Michelle added, "It's easy to tell which students are a part of the STARS program when they are among other freshman groups."

When asked about the University's involvement with African centered rites of passage, Michelle explained, "The university provided funds and place; that's it! Rites are too serious and sacred to be played with. We referred to the experts in the community who were familiar with and certified in African centered rites of passage." Michelle reiterates the need for culturally specific rites in order to develop the true self.

Though it is too early to draw sound conclusions about the effects of an African centered rites of passage process on the academic performance of the new STARS, there is evidence to suggest that rites have made a positive difference. However, there is a small body of literature which examines culturally based socialization.

Culturally Based Socialization and Education

In a study concerned with reforming the education of blacks in South Africa, Ripinga (1980) suggested that the fundamental guidelines for a model of black education are contained in the coming-of-age ceremonies. He maintains that the primary goal of education is to prepare students for the "adulthood phenomenon": the meaning and experience of being an adult. Ripinga asserts that rites of passage provide a frame of reference of an idealized authentic practice of education. In a study of academically successful black college students, Southerland (1987) found that high perceived race-(cultural)-related socialization is associated with more positive self-concept and higher Black consciousness. Since all the students in this study were academically successful, Southerland's research also implies that African self-(Black)-consciousness does not necessarily come at the expense of academic achievement. Students who developed a high sense of self were educated, while the others were "well schooled." Culture-related socialization (African centered rites of passage) fosters education *and* personality development (Deitcher, 1985).

This is consistent with studies that examined rites as a basis for conceptualizing new information (or information from outside one's present frame of reference). In a study of Basanga people in Zaire, Persons (1990) argues that the rites of passage process is key to the development of their worldview. In a similar study examining interaction between Christian religious education and sociocultural context in Ghana, Anderson-Mensah (1993) concludes that the Protestant churches in Ghana should construct a new paradigm of confirmation education. He states:

> The rites of passage provide an appropriate cultural base for a new framework for confirmation which allows the youth to be socialized into Christian beliefs, values and attitudes within their socio-cultural context, thus enabling the youth to acknowledge the validity of their own cultural experiences.

The African centered rites of passage process puts an individual into a context of a "larger whole" (Dorsa, 1994). By building bonds between family, community, African heritage, and the cosmos (the larger whole), a student is provided the type of cultural frame that Ogbu (1991) states is important for academic success.

Conclusion

I maintain that a sense of self is an essential part of an education. It is through the self that one creates meaning and determines actions. The process of discovery and appraisal of one's talents, character, relationship to the cosmos, and purpose is the basis for one's sense of self. The development of self-consciousness becomes the criterion for determining (1) intelligence, the means by which one strategizes to execute purpose, and (2) self-control, the ability to follow one's strategy (Dewey, 1938/1963). Sense of self provides the basis by which one critically examines the world and interprets information. However, the construction of self is not totally internal and independent of external influences. A culture must transmit the basic necessities for developing self. In this study I affirm that the purpose of rites of passage is to provide rituals and ceremonies that reflect the heritage and philosophies (collective wisdom) of a culture/society, in order to transmit the basic tenets for positive self-development. Somè (1994, p. 68) describes it as "gaining access to the memory of my life purpose." This strongly implies that there must be high cultural synchronization between the heritage of self and the cultural base of the rites of passage, or the meanings will be distorted (Hill, 1992; Perkins, 1986; Warfield-Coppock, 1992, 1994). For example, the Bar Mitzvah has little significance in a Hindu tradition. Accepting responsibility, developing and fulfilling purpose, and understanding one's place in a society may be themes common to various cultures; however, the philosophies and ethos that frame such themes are often different. This is also true for education (Erchak, 1992; Hamil, 1990).

Given the rites of passage process, the formal educational system is the preparation stage that prepares members for the maintenance and development of society in the United States. As with other aspects of rites of passage, education must be relative to the student (Biko, 1978; Boykin, 1986; Dewey, 1938/1963; Du Bois, 1903/1965; Freire, 1970; Hale-Benson, 1986; Kunjufu, 1984; Shujaa, 1994; Woodson, 1933/1990). A student must be able to interpret and transform the information presented in order to make a school experience educative (Akoto, 1992; Biko, 1978; Butchart, 1994; Dewey, 1938/1963; Frankl, 1962; Freire, 1970; Gowin, 1981; Grambs, 1965; Hale-Benson, 1986; Karenga, 1995; Nyerere, 1967; Shade, 1989; Somè, 1994; Warfield-Coppock, 1992; Wilson, 1993).

Consider Shade's (1989) Information Processing Model (p. 27). The input and organization/conceptual/ discrimination stages are functions of self (Akbar, 1985; Asante, 1987; Boykin, 1986; Dewey, 1938/1963; Erchak, 1992; Freire, 1970; Grambs, 1965; Hamil, 1990; Karenga, 1995; Nyerere, 1967; Rogers, 1951; Somè, 1994; Wilson, 1987). Each cycle through this model will modify the filter and memory, which will influence conceptualization and cognitive performance, and thus the self (Dewey, 1938/1963). If a filter and memory are not transmitted by culture, then the values and ethos of the experiences and information will construct them (Afrik, 1993; Ani, 1994; Grambs, 1965; Wilson, 1993; Woodson, 1933/1990). This poses little problem when there is high cultural synchronization between the values and ethos of the information and the heritage of the self being developed (Boykin, 1986;

Irvine, 1991). However, in the case of African American students this is typically not true. The tenets for developing a positive African sense of self are not present in mainstream schooling in the United States (Boykin, 1986; Du Bois, 1903/1965; Durgans, 1992; Hale-Benson, 1986; Woodson, 1933/1990).

Because African American students often have low cultural synchronization with the values and ethos of the curriculum and the school systems, it is critical for African American students to be insulated from the Eurocentric hegemonic beliefs about people of African descent. Information laced with Eurocentric hegemonic values must be transformed to useful and meaningful concepts. African American students equipped with a sense of self (African cultural filters and memory, purpose, and responsibility) are enabled to transform and interpret information so that school experiences can be educative (Obiakor, 1995). African centered rites of passage aid in the development of the cultural filters and memory necessary to build a context in which an African American student can make meaning (Somè, 1994). Consequently, African centered rites of passage complement the goals of education: to transmit from one generation to the next the accumulated wisdom and knowledge of the society, and to prepare the young people for their future membership in the society and their active participation in its maintenance and development (Nyerere, 1967). They not only encourage the development of a sense of self; rites foster other academic success factors that many scholars have identified as being important, such as parental and community involvement, support, and expectations; a sense of controlling one's destiny/internal locus of control; fictive kinship; self-control; and purpose (Akoto, 1992; Dewey, 1938/1963; Fordham, 1988, 1991; Goggins & Lindbeck, 1986; Green & Wright, 1992; Kafele, 1991; Kunjufu, 1984, 1985, 1986; Levine & Havighurst, 1992).

Also, this study strongly suggests that the measurement of academic success should use the same cultural aspects that shape filters, memory, and expectations (Erchak, 1992; Freire, 1970; Hamil, 1990; Karenga, 1995; Nyerere, 1967; Somè, 1994; Wilson, 1987). In other words, the African American community, especially families, should develop standards by which to determine academic success. These standards should foster the development and maintenance of the African American family, community, and heritage. These standards should be taught as essential criteria for development and recognition within family and community—African centered rites of passage.

What does this mean for Parents, Educators, and Scholars?

Parents

We must see education as a process that starts long before a child is sent to school. The foundations of the educative process lie within the cultural context, a context which *we* must build for our children. The values, rituals, and ceremonies which comprise the African centered rites of passage provide the necessary tools to construct the cultural context. The power of the rites process derives from implied assumptions and the relationships they foster. The major assumptions which frame the African centered rites of passage process are:

1. Every person has a built-in capacity to succeed.
2. Every person is born with a driving intent to express this capacity.
3. We are one with the Cosmos (the Creator and the creation).
4. The Creator does not design for failure.
   (adapted from Mensah, 1991)

58

These assumptions provide the impetus for individuals to seek purpose and meaning. It is the responsibility of the family and community to guide the individual through the African centered rites of passage in order to find their own vision and role in the Cosmos. The rites process starts at birth and continues to ancestry. As one moves from infancy to childhood, from childhood to adolescence, from adolescence to adulthood, and so on until ancestry, each transition corresponds with a higher level of consciousness about one's place in the Cosmos. This is the awesome power of the rites process.

As Sun-tzu implied, a sense of self is necessary for knowing who the enemy is. A sense of self is the basis of the ability to determine which experiences, values, and people are harmful (mis-educative) and which are helpful (educative). Therefore, an individual who has entered into a process which clarifies the self and purpose (rites of passage) is being prepared for education. Specifically, African centered rites of passage aid in the development of an authentic self within a cultural context which is consistent with the African American heritage. Furthermore, it is dangerous to assume that a school system will properly educate our children without parental and community involvement. If we do not raise them up in the way they should go, then they are at the mercy of this society. Consequently, it is imperative that *we* provide our children with African centered rites of passage.

Educators

We must see knowledge as a social construction that reflects the perspectives, values, and experiences of the people and cultures that constructed it. Knowledge is not a static artifact, but a dynamic debate among its creators and users. Hence, classrooms should be a forum for discussing knowledge-active "meaning making" (Goggins,

1995). This is in stark contrast to the traditional Tyler rationale, the banking concept to which Freire (1970) refers. Those who participate in this mind-numbing, consciousness-draining exercise should be referred to as trainers rather than educators.

Education when done properly will empower students to fulfill purpose, as determined through their sense of self. This requires an educational process that is not isolated from the cultural context in which the self is found. Given the definition of education, the curriculum should engage students in the development and maintenance of their communities. Schools should encourage family members and community elders to participate in real ways with the activities in the school. Also, schools can provide a place for various community activities and events. These are some of the ways in which educators can be catalysts[4] to the rites of passage process.

Scholars

Until now, most scholarship concerning African Americans' involvement with the educational system has described problems, characterized those who have been successful, or focused on particular factors. Relatively little focused on real solutions, in particular, solutions that can be implemented by the student, the family, and the community.

Theories and strategies for academic success need to be identified that consider the development, socialization, and enculturation of youth, paradigms and values that shape education, and academic success factors. Recently there has been a rerecognition of the importance of rituals, ceremonies, and role definition in the development

---

[4.] I use *catalyst* to suggest that schools must not be the primary agent in the rites process, unless they are of the same cultural context. Family members and community elders must guide and participate in the process.

of productive people. In this study I maintain that additional research should examine processes rather than individual factors. Most academic factors, such as socioeconomic status, teacher expectations, self-esteem, and so forth, are not significant in isolation. African centered rites of passage tend to bring these factors together.

The literature describing how to develop and implement African centered rites of passage is very limited. Scholarly research studying African centered rites of passage is almost nonexistent. More is needed.

For more information about African Centered Rites of Passage,

I suggest the following books:

Benjamin, T. G. (1993). *Boys to Men.* Indianapolis, IN: Heaven On Earth Publishing House.

Hare, N, & Hare, J. (1985). *Bringing the Black Boy to Manhood: The Passage.* San Francisco: Black Think Tank.

Hill, P., Jr. (1992). *Coming of Age: African American Male Rites of Passage.* Chicago: African American Images.

Lewis, M. C. (1988). *Herstory: Black Female Rites of Passage.* Chicago: African American Images

Perkins, U. E. (1986). *Harvesting New Generations: The Positive Development of Black Youth.* Chicago: Third World Press.

Somè, M. (1993). *Rituals: Power, Healing, and Community.* Portland, OR: Swan, Raven

Warfield-Coppock, N. (1990). *Afrocentric Theory and Applications, Volume 1: Adolescent Rites of Passage.* Washington, D.C.: Baobab Associates.

I have also compiled a list of organizations and people throughout the country who are participating in African centered rites of passage. If you would like a copy you may reach me, Lathardus Goggins, II at:

THE MAWASI COMPANY

P.O. Box 1852   (330) 836-1199 (voice/fax)
Akron, OH 44309   ujima@aol.com   (e-mail)

Other Related Issues

I have discussed aspects of African centered rites of passage and related matters, on which further research should be conducted. These are some of the issues.

Integration, Segregation, and Assimilation

With the increased scholarly examination and development of African centered philosophies, some have argued that Afrocentricity is ultimately detrimental. Wiley (1994) suggests "we" (African Americans) are a different "kind"–we are out of Africa. We are children of the New World. His perception is that African centered thinking would lead to separatist tendencies and segregation from opportunities. In terms of education, the academic success of African American students is a function of the extent of their integration into American society. Wortham (1995) suggests that "Afro-centrism is not the answer for black students in American society." Her views severely misrepresent African centered thought and ethos. Wortham asserts that education in a diverse and integrated society should teach general principles instead of African cultural specifics. I would agree that integration is an important factor in academic success, but not as integration is often practiced, "the right to assimilate." Blacks have the right to do as whites do, as suggested by Wortham. As I have used *integration*, it is to understand and fulfill a purpose within a diverse group, with cooperation among various groups of people. There is an implied understanding that each group has something to give to the whole: a unique genius. Even those who stress the importance of multiculturalism must recognize the importance of each group developing self. If this is not recognized, then *multiculturalism* is doomed to be the next politically correct term for *assimilation*. Research by Cross, Parham, & Helms (1991) suggests that development of self-consciousness can lead to more humanistic, integrated behavior.

Various Nigrescence (Black Identity Development) models have maintained that there are five stages to Black consciousness: (1) Pre-encounter, (2) Encounter, (3) Immersion-Emersion, (4) Internalization, and (5) Internalization-Commitment. These models suggest that Black identity/African self-consciousness is a function of the event in which one can no longer deny one's Blackness. As is often implied, the event is traumatic and negative in nature: "having a rug pulled from under you" (Cross, Parham, & Helms, 1991). Next, this person immerses himself/herself in a search for African identity. The Nigrescence models also state that a person in this stage of consciousness will tend to develop a counterculture or militant reference to the mainstream. Unfortunately, few move into Internalization and Internalization-Commitment, the fourth and fifth stages of consciousness. I would argue that the nature of the encounter has a major effect on the development of consciousness. As most often described, the development of African self-consciousness is a reaction, not a proaction. As mentioned before, to develop a sense of self in opposition to something is to be centered by that something.

Families, churches, and community organizations that provide African centered rites of passage as an essential healthy part of the development of a person, just as proper nutrition and exercise are important, provide a proactive and positive encounter. There is no old self to reconcile, nor is there resentment for being taught lies. I would argue that family-based, community-linked African centered rites of passage would more likely develop a fourth stage of development of African self-consciousness, which is necessary for true integration. As one elder stated, and many scholars maintain: "Authentic self allows for authentic interaction with others."

Culture and Race

This study and the relevant literature strongly assert that culture is learned. Cultural values and ethos are transmitted through the evaluation of experiences, a primarily cognitive process. However, where the issues of the black race are concerned, it seems that many people believe that culture is a function of race, primarily genetic. Unfortunately, many in the African American community have also adopted this belief.

One evidence of such thinking is the location of Black studies programs. These programs are overwhelmingly concentrated at predominately white institutions. Ironically, the institutions with the largest concentration of African American students do not typically have strong Black studies programs. There are a number of reasons for this discrepancy. One is the notion that African American students at HBCUs will pick up a sense of the African American experience. True, there are some unique cultural aspects present in such a situation. But can a group of people, many of whom have not studied their heritage, produce meaningful culture? Most predominately white institutions evidently believe not; thus, they require a course on European/Western culture development.

A belief that race equals culture is a product of a racist and oppressive system (Maquet, 1967/1972). As Freire, (1970) stated, the projection of absolute ignorance onto the oppressed is a tendency of the oppressor. In the United States, the mainstream used race as justification for oppression. Being black (genetic) is the reason for ignorance. Ignorance (cognitive) is the reason for deficient culture (performance).

Many African Americans have taken issue with the Race/Genetics -> Ignorance/Cognitive -> Culture/Performance assumption. To do so, African American scholars and leaders have attacked the assumption of ignorance and deficiency by providing examples to the contrary. However, many have accepted the connection between race and culture. Consequently, genetic characteristics have often been used as criteria to determine culture. Thick lips and nose, tightly curled hair, big butt, and dark skin have often been used as determinants for African self-consciousness. Of course how one values such characteristics *may* reflect the frame of reference, but having such characteristics is not equivalent to having an African centered frame of reference. Culture should be seen as deliberate and conscious, demanding a conscious and deliberate transmission to the next generation (Hill, 1992; Kunjufu, 1985; Perkins, 1986; Somè, 1994).

REFERENCES

Afrik, M. H. T. (1993). *The Future of Afrikan American Education: A Practitioner's View.* Chicago: Council of Independent Black Institutions.

Akbar, N. (1985). *The Community of Self.* Tallahassee, FL: Mind Productions & Associates.

Akoto, K. A. (1992). *Nation Building: Theory and Practice in African Centered Education.* Washington D.C.: Pan African World Institute.

American Association of Colleges for Teacher Education. (1989). *Rate III Teaching teachers: Facts & figures.* Washington D.C.: AACTE.

Andersen-Mensah, R. A. (1993). *Towards the Contextualization of Religious Education: Rites of Passage as Processes of Socialization in Contextual Religious Education.* Unpublished doctoral dissertation, Presbyterian School of Christian Education, Richmond, VA.

Ani, M. (1994). *Yurugu: An African Centered Critique of European Cultural Thought and Behavior.* Trenton, NJ: Africa World Press.

Asante, M. K. (1987). *The Afrocentric Idea.* Philadelphia: Temple Press.

Benjamin, T. G. (1993). *Boys to Men.* Indianapolis, IN: Heaven On Earth Publishing House.

Biko, S. (1978). *I Write What I Like.* New York: Harper & Row.

Bond, H. M. (1966). *The Education of the Negro in the American Social Order.* New York: Octagon Books.

Boykin, A. W. (1986). The triple quandary and the Afro-American children. In U. Neisser (Ed.), *The School Achievement of Minority Children.* (pp. 57–92). Hillsdale, NJ: Lawrence Erlbaum Associates.

Butchart, R. E. (1994). Outthinking and Outflanking the Owners of the World: An Historiography of the African American Struggle for Education. In M. J. Shujaa *(Ed.), Too Much Schooling, Too Little Education: A Paradox of Black Life in White Societies.* (pp. 85–122). Trenton, NJ: Africa World Press.

Cohen, D. (1991). *The Circle of Life: Rituals from the Human Family Album.* San Francisco: HarperCollins.

Cress-Welsing, F. (1991). *The Isis Papers.* Chicago: Third World Press.

Current, R. N. (1963). *The Lincoln Nobody Knows.* New York: Hill and Wang.

DaSilva, B., Finkelstein, M., Loshin, A., & Sandifer, J. A. (1969). *The Afro-American in United States History.* New York: Globe Book Company.

Deitcher, H. (1985). *The Rites of Passage: An Instructional Guide for Yeshiva High School Teachers (New York).* Unpublished doctoral dissertation, Yeshiva University, New York.

Dewey, J. (1938/1963). *Experience and Education.* New York: Collier Books.

Dorsa, D. (1994). *The Importance of Ritual to Children.* Unpublished doctoral dissertation, California Institute of Integral Studies, San Francisco, CA.

Du Bois, W. E. B. (1903/1965). *The Souls of Black Folk.* In *Three Negro Classics* (pp. 209–389). New York: Avon.

Durgans, K. (1992). *African American Self-consciousness and African American Students Attending Predominantly White Universities,* Unpublished doctoral dissertation, Western Michigan University, Kalamazoo.

Erchak, G. M. (1992). *The Anthropology of Self and Behavior.* New Brunswick, NJ: Rutgers University Press.

Estelh, K. (1994). *The African American Almanac (6th ed).* Detroit: Gale Research.

Filler, L. (1960). *The Crusade Against Slavery 1830–1860.* New York: Harper & Row.

Fleming, J. (1991). *Blacks in College.* San Francisco: Jossey-Bass Publishers.

Fordham, S. (1988). Racelessness as a factor in black students' school success: Pragmatic strategy or pyrrhic victory? *Harvard Educational Review 58* (1).

Fordham, S. (1991). Peer-proofing academic competition among black adolescents: "Acting white" Black American style. In C. E. Sleeter (Ed.), *Empowerment Through Multicultural Education* (pp. 69–93). Albany, NY: State University of New York Press.

Frankl, V. (1962). *Man's Search for Meaning*. Boston: Beacon Press.

Fraser, G. (1994). *Success Runs in Our Race*. New York: William Morrow.

Frazier, E. F. (1973). The failure of the Negro intellectual. In Joyce A. Ladner (Ed.), *The Death of White Sociology* (pp. 52–66). New York: Vintage Books.

Freire, P. (1970). *Pedagogy of the oppressed*. New York: Continuum Publishing.

Garibaldi, A. M. (1992a). Educating and motivating African American males to succeed. *Journal of Negro Education, 61*, 4–11.

Garibaldi, A. M. (1992b). Preparing teachers for culturally diverse classrooms. In M. E. Dilworth (Ed.), *Diversity in Teacher Education* (pp. 23-39). San Francisco: Jossey-Bass Publishers.

Gary, L., & Booker, C. (1992). Empowering African Americans to achieve academic success. *Urban Education, 76*, 50–52.

Gerardi, S. (1990). Academic self-concept as a predictor of academic success among minority and low-socio-economic-status students. *Journal of College Student Development, 31*, 402–407.

Gibson, M. A., & Ogbu, J. U. (1991). *Minority Status and Schooling: A Comparative Study of Immigrant and Involuntary Minorities*. New York: Garland Press.

Goggins, E. (1995). Multicultural perspectives in secondary education. In L. Goggins II (Chair), *3rd Annual African American History Month Panel Discussion*, Canton, OH.

Goggins, E., & Lindbeck, J. S. (1986). High school science enrollment of black students. *Journal of Research in Science Teaching, 23*, 251–262.

Goldschmidt, W. (1977). *Exploring the Ways of Mankind (3rd ed.)*. New York: Holt, Rinehart, and Winston.

Goode, K. (1969). *From Africa to the United States and then . . . : A Concise Afro-American History*. Glenview, IL: Scott, Foresman.

Gore, W. J. (1964). *Administrative Decision-making: A Heuristic Model*. New York: John Wiley & Sons.

Gowin, D. B. (1981). *Educating*. Ithaca, NY: Cornell University Press.

Grams, J. D. (1965). The self-concept: Basis for reeducation of Negro Youth. In W. Kvaraceus (Ed.), *Negro Self-concept* (pp. 11-52). New York: McGraw-Hill.

Green, R. L., & Wright D. L. (1992). African American Males: Demographic Study and Analysis. In B. W. Austin (Ed.), *What a Piece of Work is Man! A Discussion of Issues Affecting African American Men and Boys,* (pp. 27–78). W. K. Kellogg Foundation.

Hale-Benson, J. (1986). *Black Children: Their Roots, Culture, and Learning Styles.* Baltimore, MD: Johns Hopkins University Press.

Hamil, J. F. (1990). *Ethno-logic: The Anthropology of Human Reasoning.* Urbana: University of Illinois Press.

Hare, N. (1973). The challenge of a Black scholar. In Joyce A. Ladner (Ed.), *The Death of White Sociology* (pp. 67–78). New York: Vintage Books.

Hare, N., & Hare, J. (1985). *Bringing the Black Boy to Manhood: The Passage.* San Francisco: The Black Think Tank.

Harrell, J. (1979). Analyzing Black coping styles: A supplemental diagnostic system. *Journal of Black Psychology 5,* 99–108.

Harris, S. R. (1993). *The African American Graduate Experience: The Relationship Among Spirituality, Racial/Cultural Awareness, and Connectedness with Adaptation at a Predominantly White Institution.* Unpublished doctoral dissertation, University of Cincinnati, Cincinnati, OH.

Hill, P., Jr. (1992). *Coming of Age: African American Male Rites of Passage.* Chicago: African American Images.

Hilliard, A. G. III, Williams, L., & Damali, N. (1987). *The Teachings of Ptahhotep: The Oldest Book in the World.* Atlanta: Blackwood Press.

Irvine, J. J. (1991). *Black Students and School Failure.* New York: Praeger Publishers.

Johnson, R. E. (1993). *Factors in the Academic Success of African American College Males (African American),* Unpublished doctoral dissertation, University of South Carolina, Columbia.

Kafele, B. K. (1991). *A Black Parent's Handbook to Educating Your Children (Outside of the Classroom)*. Jersey City, NJ: Baruti Publishing.

Karenga, M. (1994). *Introduction to Black Studies*. Los Angeles: University of Sankore Press.

Karenga, M. (1995). The Black Man and the Kinetic Process of Surge to Raise up to Carry and Rejoin. In P. E. Abercrombe (Chair), *Tenth Annual Black Man's Think Tank*. Cincinnati, OH.

Keto, C. T. (1991). *The Africa-centered Perspective of History: An Introduction*. Laurel Springs, NJ: K. A. Publishers.

Knowles, L. L., & Prewitt, K. (1969). *Institutional Racism in America*. Englewoods Cliffs, N.J.: Prentice-Hall.

Kohn, A. (1994). The truth about self-esteem. *Phi Delta Kappan, 76*, 272–283.

Kunjufu, J. (1984). *Developing Positive Self-Images and Discipline in Black Children*. Chicago: African American Images.

Kunjufu, J. (1985). *Countering the Conspiracy to Destroy Black Boys*. Chicago: African American Images.

Kunjufu, J. (1986). *Motivating and Preparing Black Youth for Success*. Chicago: African American Images.

Lee, C. (1984). An investigation of Psychosocial variables related to academic success for rural black adolescents. *The Journal of Negro Education, 53*, 424–434.

Lent, R., Brown, S., & Larkin, K. (1986). Self-efficacy in the prediction of academic performance and perceived career options. *The American Psychological Association, 33*, 265–269.

Levine, D. U., & Havighurst, R. J. (1992). *Society and Education*. Boston: Allyn and Bacon.

Lewis, M. C. (1988). *Herstory: Black Female Rites of Passage*. Chicago: African American Images.

Loh, J. (1994, December 18). Death of the Ku Klux Klan. *The Beacon Journal*.

Macias, C. (1989). American Indian academic success: The role of indigenous learning strategies. *Journal of American Indian Education-Special Issue, 43*–152.

Macintosh, J. (1995). The human tribe. In M. Beynon (Producer), *The Human Animal*. London: British Broadcasting Corporation.

Majors, R., & Billson, J. M. (1992). *Cool Pose*. New York: Touchstone.

Maquet, J. (1967/1972). *Africanity*. Joan R. Rayfield, Trans. New York: Oxford University Press.

Marsh, C., & Willis, G. (1995). *Curriculum: Alternative Approaches, Ongoing Issues*. Englewood Cliffs, NJ: Merrill.

McClendon, R. C. (1995). As to the need for recruitment. In Task Force for Quality Education, *Town Meeting*. Akron, OH.

McConnell, B. (1989). Education as a cultural process: The interaction between community and classroom in fostering learning. In J. Allen & J. M. Mason (Eds.), *Risk Makers, Risk Takers, Risk Breakers: Reducing the Risk for Young Literacy Learners* (pp. 201–211). Portsmouth, NH: Heinemann Educational Books.

McMillan, J., & Reed, D. (1994). At-risk students and resiliency: Factors contributing to academic success. *The Clearing House 67*, 137–140.

M.E.C.C.A. (n.d.). *African Americans Resurrect Rites of Passage Through a Comprehensive Family & Community Development Model*.

Mensah, A. (1991). *Preliminal Materials for the Development of a Rites of Passage Course*. Milwaukee, WI: Mensah Publications.

Montgomery, A., Rossi, R., Legters, N., McDill, E., McPartland, J., & Stringfield, S. (1993). *Educational Reforms and Students at Risk: A Review of the Current State of the Art. (Shipping list No. 94-0080-M)*. Washington, D.C.: U.S. Department of Education, U.S. Government Printing Office.

Nyerere, J. K. (1967). *Education for Self-Reliance*. Dar es Salaam, Tanzania.

Obiakor, F. E. (1995). Self-concept model for African American students in special educational settings. In B. A. Ford, F. E. Obiakor, & J. A. Patton (Eds.), *Effective Education of African American Exceptional Learners*. Austin, TX: PRO-ED.

O'Callaghan, K., & Bryant, C. (1990). Noncognitive variables: A key to Black American academic success at a military academy? *Journal of College Student Development, 31,* 121–126.

Ogbu, J. U. (1974). *The Next Generation: An Ethnography of Education in an Urban Neighborhood.* New York: Academic Press.

Ogbu, J. U. (1986). Consequences of the American caste system. In U. Neisser (Ed.), *The School Achievement of Minority Children,* (pp. 19-56). Hillsdale, NJ: Lawrence Erlbaum Associates.

Ogbu, J. U. (1991). Immigrant and involuntary minorities in comparative perspective. In M. A. Gibson & J. U. Ogbu (Eds.), *Minority Status and Schooling: A Comparative Study of Immigrant and Involuntary Minorities.* (pp. 3-33). New York: Garland Press.

Patterson, C. H. (1986). *Theories of Counseling and Psychotherapy.* New York: Harper & Row.

Patton, J. M. (1993). Psychological assessment of gifted and talented African Americans. In J. H. Stanfield & D. H. Rutledge (Eds.), *Race and Ethnicity in Research Methods* (pp. 198-216). Newbury Park, CA: Sage Publications.

Perkins, U. E. (1986). *Harvesting New Generations: The Positive Development of Black Youth.* Chicago: Third World Press.

Petes, M. (1974). *The Ebony Book of Black Achievement.* Chicago: Johnson Publishing.

Pinkney, A. (1975). *Black Americans.* Englewood Cliffs, NJ: Prentice-Hall.

Powell, T. (1992). *The Persistence of Racism in America.* Lanham, MD: University Press of America.

Quinn, W. H., Newfield, N. A., & Protinsky, H. O. (1985). Rites of passage in families with adolescents. *Family Process, 24,* 101–111.

Ripinga, S. S. (1980). *Adulthood in Pedagogical Perspective and its Significance in Designing a Model for Black Education.* Unpublished doctoral dissertation, University of South Africa.

Rogers, C. R. (1951). *Client-Centered Therapy: Its Current Practice, Implications, and Theory.* Boston: Houghton Mifflin.

Russakoff, D. (1995, February 9). Rutgers head struggles to save job. *Washington Post.*

Salaam, M. H. (1992). *The Relationship of African Cultural Consciousness and Self-esteem on the Academic Achievement of African American Students.* Unpublished doctoral dissertation, University of California, Los Angeles.

Shade, B. (1989). Cognitive style, what is it? Afro-American cognitive patterns. In B. Shade (Ed.), *Culture, Style, and the Educative Process* (pp. 87-115). Springfield, IL: Charles C. Thomas.

Shaffer, D. R. (1993). *Developmental Psychology: Childhood and Adolescence.* Pacific Grove, CA: Brooks/Cole.

Shere, C. (1993). *A Participant Observation Case Study Using Van Gennep's Rites of Passage Theory at a "Summer Transitional Program."* Unpublished doctoral dissertation, Columbia University Teachers College, New York.

Shujaa, M. J. (Ed.)(1994). *Too Much Schooling, Too Little Education: A Paradox of Black Life in White Societies.* Trenton, NJ: Africa World Press.

Somè, M. (1993). *Rituals: Power, Healing, and Community.* Portland, OR: Swan/Raven.

Somè, M. (1994). Rites of passage. *Utne Reader, 64,* 67–68.

Southerland, D. L. (1987). *Self-Concept, Black Consciousness, and Race-Related Socialization in Academically Successful Black College Students,* Unpublished doctoral dissertation, University of Cincinnati, Cincinnati, OH.

Sowa, C., Thomson, M., & Bennett, C. (1989). Prediction and improvement of academic performance for high-risk black college students. *Journal of Multicultural Counseling and Development, 17,* 14–22.

Sowell, T. (1986). *Education: Assumptions Versus History.* Stanford, CA: Hoover Press.

Spaights, E., Kenner, D., & Dixon, H. (1986). The relationship of self-concept and the academic success of black students in white institutions of higher education. *Journal of Instructional Psychology, 13,* 111–121.

Spindler, G., & Spindler, L. (1990). *The American Cultural Dialogue and Its Transmission.* London: Falmer Press.

Stampp, K. M. (1956). *The Peculiar Institution.* New York: Alfred A. Knopf.

Steinfield, M. (1972). *Our Racist Presidents: From Washington to Nixon.* San Ramon, CA: Consensus Publishers.

Stokes, J. E. (1994). *The Influence of Race Socialization on the Group Identity and Self-Esteem of African American Youth.* Unpublished doctoral dissertation, University of California, Riverside.

Sun-tzu. (6th Cent. B.C./1988). *The Art of War.* Thomas Cleary, Trans. Boston: Shamblaala Publications.

Toppin, E. A. (1971). *A Biographical History of Blacks in America Since 1528.* New York: David McKay.

Tracey, T. J., & Sedlacek, W. E. (1985). The relationship of noncognitive variables to academic success: A longitudinal comparison by race. *Journal of College Student Personnel, 26,* 405–410.

Tracey, T. J., & Sedlacek, W. E. (1987). Prediction of college graduation using noncognitive variables by race. *Measurement and Evaluation in Counseling and Development, 19,* 177–184.

Ullman, A. D. (1965). *Sociocultural Foundations of Personality.* Boston: Houghton Mifflin.

Van Gennep, A. (1908/1960). *The Rites of Passage.* Monika B. Solon and Gabrielle L. Caffee, Trans. Chicago: University of Chicago Press.

Wambach, C. (1993). Motivational themes and academic success of at-risk freshmen. *Journal of Developmental Education, 16,* 8–37.

Warfield-Coppock, N. (1992). The rites of passage movement: A resurgence of African-Centered practices for socializing African American youth. *Journal of Negro Education, 61,* 471–482.

Warfield-Coppock, N. (1994). The rites of passage: Extending education into the African American community. In M. J. Shujaa (Ed.), *Too Much Schooling, Too Little Education: A Paradox of Black Life in White Societies* (pp. 375–393). Trenton, NJ: Africa World Press.

West, C. (1994). *Race Matters*. New York: Vintage.

Williams, G. W. (1886/1968). *History of the Negro Race in America 1619-1880*. New York: Arno Press.

Wilson, A. N. (1987). *The Developmental Psychology of the Black Child*. New York: Africana Research Publications.

Wilson, A. N. (1993). *The Falsification Of Afrikan Consciousness*. New York: Afrikan World InfoSystems.

Woodson, C. G. (1933/1990). *The Mis-education of the Negro*. Trenton, NJ: Africa World Press.

Wylen, S. M. (1989). *Settings of Silver: An Introduction to Judaism*. New York: Paulist Press.

Yellow Robe, R. (1969). *An Album of the American Indian*. New York: Franklin Watts.

Young, B., & Sowa, C. (1992). Predictors of academic success for Black student athletes. *Journal of College Student Development, 33*, 319–324.

NOTES